The Work of the
Sunday School Superintendent

The Work of the
Sunday School Superintendent

Idris W. Jones

Revised by Ruth L. Spencer

Judson Press ® Valley Forge

LIBRARY OF CONGRESS CATALOGING-IN-PUBLICATION DATA
Jones, Idris W.
The work of the Sunday school superintendent / by Idris W. Jones; revised
by Ruth L. Spencer. — Rev. ed.
p.   cm.
Original ed. published under title: The superintendent plans his work.
1956.
ISBN 0-8170-1229-X
1. Sunday school superintendents. I. Spencer, Ruth L.
II. Jones, Idris W. Superintendent plans his work. III. Title.
BV1531.J58 1994
268'.1—dc20   94-3591

Printed in the U.S.A.
94 95 96 97 98 99 00 01   25 24 23 22 21 20 19 18

Contents

Statement of the Christian Education Goal

The goal of the church's educational ministry is that all persons

—be aware of God through God's self-disclosure, especially God's redeeming love as revealed in Jesus Christ, and

—be enabled by the Holy Spirit to respond in faith and love so that they may

—become new persons in Christ;

—know who they are and what their human situation means;

—grow as children of God rooted in the Christian community;

—live in obedience to the will of God in every relationship;

—fulfill their common vocation in the world, and

—abide in the Christian hope.

Chapter 1

The General Superintendent Views the Work

Every church *wants* a good Sunday church school. What is more, every church, no matter how large or how small, can *have* an effective Sunday school. But if it is to have such a school, it must put forth the effort that is required.

Many factors enter into the building of an effective Sunday school, but one key factor is the superintendent. The church, or its board of Christian education, may plan a splendid program to be achieved through its Sunday school; it may analyze the opportunities for enlisting, training, and equipping teachers; and it may face questions about curriculum, grading, time schedules, and space allotment. But it still will need a good leader to unify its policies, to see that they are carried out, and to evaluate their effectiveness. The superintendent is that person and will at all times work in close cooperation with the board and other persons associated with Christian education. The general superintendent is usually elected by the church. Whether the school is large or small, the superintendent has responsibilities in connection with students, teachers, curriculum, space, equipment, and staff. These create both opportunities and problems.

In most churches the Sunday school is the principal phase of the Christian education program. In some churches it is the only organized program of Christian education. The leadership of such an organization, therefore, carries a most strategic responsibility.

The superintendent is a key person not only because of important administrative responsibilities but also because of the influences on the spiritual growth of many persons. The superintendent's life, character, and personal relationships with officers and teachers have a direct bearing upon their development and morale. The influence upon the students comes through a dual channel: directly, through personal relationships with them; indirectly, through influence upon their teachers. Thus, the superintendent is a key person both as a manager and as a spiritual leader. The person chosen by the church for this work receives the church's stamp of confidence as an administrator and as an example of the kind of Christian life in which it believes.

The superintendency demands certain other qualifications. Inasmuch as most of them grow out of the nature of the work the superintendent is called upon to perform, let us examine first the task. In a sense, the work is not set before one; it rather moves along like a constantly changing stream. A superintendent may be summoned to plunge in where the problems are thickest or may personally discover situations requiring assistance, in addition to the briefings by the pastor, director of Christian education, board of Christian education, or other informed persons. Although conditions may vary from school to school, the superintendent will find that most of the work falls within a framework of duties common to all superintendents.

There are many superintendents who have caught the thrilling vision of their opportunity, who have grasped its elements, and who have learned the dual art of "doing first things first" and "assigning responsibility."

The Superintendent's Work

The superintendent will note that six major elements are involved in the nature of the work. These are students, teachers, curriculum, equipment and space, administrative relationships, and the school's relationships with the church, parents, and community. Whether a school has twenty-five members or two thousand members, these six elements are always present. They call for separate consideration.

The Superintendent's Work Involves
Students
Teachers
Curriculum
Equipment and Space
Administrative Relationships
The School's Relationships

1. *Students:* The Sunday school exists to present the Good News of Jesus Christ in such appealing fashion that children, youth, and adults will be nurtured and grow in the Christian faith. It exists to encourage each student to make a personal commitment to Christ and to be empowered to live as a faithful disciple.

Without students a Sunday school would not exist. Students of all ages, therefore, are the superintendent's first concern. In working with students, the superintendent is confronted with these questions:

a. How can we find and enlist new students?

b. How can we welcome these new members so that they will want to continue coming?

c. How will our students be grouped into classes?

d. How can we increase regularity of attendance on the part of those who are members?

e. How can we win persons to an acceptance of Jesus Christ as Lord and Savior?

f. How can we develop discipleship in the students?

g. How can we evaluate the influence of the school upon the students?

h. How can we involve members of the Sunday school in the total life of the church?

2. *Teachers:* If a school cannot exist without students to be taught, persons cannot be taught without teachers to instruct and guide them in their spiritual growth. Securing teachers, therefore, will always be one of the superintendent's major concerns. Even if the school is fully staffed for the present, there will be concern with training available personnel for the future. The superintendent will work with the board of Christian education in the enlistment and development of workers.

The teaching staff, as a factor in the superintendent's work, presents these questions:

a. How many teachers do we need and for what age groups do we need them?

b. Where can we find such present or potential teachers?

c. How can we enlist these persons as teachers?

d. How can we help them to acquire the skills that will enable them to enjoy their work and to grow in effectiveness as teachers?

e. How can we best honor their commitment to do God's work as we offer encouragement and inspiration?

3. *Curriculum:* The teaching tripod rests on three legs: the student, the teacher, and that which is taught—the curriculum. Between what the teacher is consciously attempting to teach and what the student actually learns there may be a great chasm. This chasm can be bridged in two ways: through the improved

effectiveness of the teacher as a Christian leader and through the provision of better curriculum materials.

The following questions have to do with the curriculum. The superintendent will find it helpful to discuss them with the teachers, the department superintendents, and the board of Christian education.

a. What are our Christian education goals and objectives, and what do we want to have happen in the lives of our students?

b. What curriculum materials can best help us to achieve these Christian education goals?

c. How is our Sunday school curriculum correlated with the other Christian experiences of the students?

d. What place does the curriculum give to decision and growth in the Christian life?

e. How effectively is the Bible study, worship, fellowship, and service of the church related to the curriculum objectives?

f. Does the total curriculum include varied experiences that will provide for growth from one age level (or department) to another, avoid duplication, and prevent the omission of important emphases in the program?

4. *Equipment and Space:* Although the student, teacher, and curriculum are the basic elements in the teaching-learning experience, the superintendent will soon discover that other factors become important as the number of teaching-learning groups increases. When one or more new classes are created, finding adequate space and equipment may become a major administrative concern. In many churches the board of Christian education is rightly responsible for allocating space and providing needed equipment. But even where this is the case, the superintendent, as the school ad-

ministrator and an ex-officio member of the board, will be greatly concerned in all decisions relating to space and equipment. These, then, are the questions that the superintendent needs to ask:

a. What is the best use of the existing space and equipment for effective teaching, particularly as that use affects the grouping of students and the teaching opportunity?

b. What are the points of greatest need in equipment and space?

c. What practical solutions for these needs can the superintendent seek to achieve? What is needed first and how can it be procured?

d. What procedure can be used to see that the school's rooms and equipment are always kept clean and in order?

5. *The Superintendent's Administrative Relationships:* In a small Sunday school the superintendent's administrative relationships are relatively simple; in a larger school they are highly complex; in both situations they are exceedingly important. Concerning these administrative relationships, the superintendent will find it helpful to ask the following questions:

a. What persons are involved in making decisions affecting our Sunday school?

b. What is my relationship as superintendent to each of these persons or groups?

c. What is the best distribution of administrative responsibility for our school? What officers do we need?

d. How frequently and on what matters should I, as superintendent, confer with the pastor, the director of Christian education (where one is employed), the board of Christian education, and the teachers and officers of the school?

e. In what way can I best guide the planning of an effective program for our school and help in the assignment of responsibilities?

f. How can I best guide our teachers and officers in setting and achieving annual goals or objectives?

g. How can the program and the classes within the school best integrate time schedules, space, and equipment?

h. How can the program of the Sunday school best be integrated with the program of the total church and the related activities outside the church?

i. How can I keep a constant check on the program and work of the school in the light of its avowed objectives?

j. What is the nature and frequency of my report as superintendent to the church or to its board of Christian education?

k. On what occasions in church and community am I as superintendent expected to represent the school officially?

l. On what occasions do I act as the presiding officer? How can I become more effective in this responsibility?

6. *The Relationship of the Sunday School to the Church, the Parents, and the Community:* The church is constantly teaching through its many activities, even in those cases where it consciously considers its Sunday school as its only organized educational program. The school actually is but one part of that wider religious training and experience that the church provides. As the school functions, its members and leaders discover that the total church, the parents of the children and young people, and the community at large—all have an influence on the school, its personnel, and its program.

The superintendent, therefore, can strengthen

the school by finding constructive answers to these questions:

a. How can the church as a whole be helped to recognize the value of the Sunday school and the importance of its teaching program?

b. How can the work and the needs of the school be kept constantly before the church?

c. In what ways do the parents and the school cooperate in the Christian teaching program of the church?

d. What opportunities do the school and its staff have for cooperating with those from other Sunday schools in training, service, and fellowship?

e. How can the resources of the community be used to advantage in the Sunday school?

The Superintendent's Leadership

As the administrator of the Sunday school, the superintendent is cast in several roles. By temperament and training a superintendent may be better suited for some of these roles than for others. Nevertheless, all of them contribute to an effective ministry. Even when

The Superintendent Is
A Spiritual Leader
An Educator
An Administrator
An Organizer
A Leader of Worship
A Personal Counselor
A Symbol

some of these duties are delegated to others, an elementary understanding of them will be useful. Here we are thinking of the superintendent as a volunteer worker who dedicates time and ability to the educational work of the church for a period of months— even as many co-workers are also serving the church as teachers, department superintendents, youth leaders, deacons, or trustees.

1. *A Spiritual Leader:* A person who is chosen as the superintendent of the Sunday school is by virtue of that choice recognized as a spiritual leader, however modest and genuinely humble in spirit. Teachers, officers, and students will expect the superintendent to maintain the spiritual morale of the school by personal example and by manner of leadership. This includes a respect for and commitment to the task, and a sincere desire to further the Christian faith. A superintendent who considers it a privilege to serve on behalf of the church school will use every energy and talent to do the best possible job.

2. *An Educator:* The superintendent is not only a spiritual leader but also an educator. As the leader of an educational organization of the church, the superintendent will do well to learn as much as possible about the educational process. What is good teaching? What is poor teaching? What makes the difference? What is most important in the choice of curriculum materials?

In individual conferences and designated training sessions with teachers, a superintendent will find ways to help teachers gain specific teaching skills, such as the art of asking questions that will encourage students to explore ideas. These, in turn, will enable the teachers to improve the teaching-learning experiences they plan and carry out with the students. Recognizing why persons come to Sunday school, how they learn, and other educational principles, will give teachers confidence in their work and strengthen the morale of the Sunday school.

Although some who are called upon to be superintendents do not have the opportunity to take extensive training as educators, there are many things they can do to improve their leadership. Frequently the superintendent will know persons in the church or community who have done outstanding work in teaching children, youth, or adults. Usually they will be ready to help not only in training teachers but also in sharing educational insights that will assist the superintendent.

The superintendent can get help from such a book as *Basic Teacher Skills* by Richard Rusbuldt (Valley Forge: Judson Press, 1981). This book discusses in detail the basic roles of a teacher and offers easy-to-follow steps for planning the session, learning/teaching activities to accomplish session objectives, and information about how students learn. The sample lesson plans are invaluable for stimulating teachers' own creative ideas. Included is a leader's guide which can be used by the superintendent for orientation of new teachers.

3. *An Administrator:* The superintendent is an administrator responsible for carrying out the educational policies related to the work of the Sunday school. Part of this responsibility is to meet with the board of Christian education, the pastor or church director of Christian education, and the Sunday school workers to plan policies and programs. Coordinating time schedules and the best use of available space and equipment are some of their concerns. *Developing Christian Education in the Smaller Church* by Carolyn C. Brown (Nashville: Abingdon Press, 1982) provides valuable helps to guide a superintendent in these important administrative, as well as other, tasks. For example, the superintendent will make sure that there are sufficient Bibles, suitable music resources, and adequate curriculum materials; teachers and workers will know from whom they can secure other supplies, such as paper, crayons, pencils, scissors, and glue.

A good administrator not only plans one's own work but also helps teachers to see the importance of adequate planning for each session of the school. By the superintendent's example, as well as by specific suggestions, teachers will discover the thrill of better teaching achieved through proper planning.

4. *An Organizer:* The superintendent is not only an administrator fulfilling responsibilities within an organizational framework already established, but also is often an organizer confronted with new responsibilities.

For example, a rural Sunday school of approximately fifty members, in one of the midwestern states, had gone along for years with two children's classes, a youth class, and an adult class. When a nearby city began to grow, it stretched out until by the end of the decade the church was no longer rural but suburban. For some of the members this was a difficult adjustment. Fortunately, however, both the pastor and the superintendent were persons of vision. Instead of permitting the school to grow in hit-or-miss fashion, adding a class whenever the current pressure called for it, they reorganized the school on a graded basis that would allow for all foreseeable expansion. This growing church now has a board of Christian education in charge of all its educational activities, and the church itself is working to find additional space for its increased membership.

Few superintendents will run into such a major organizational change; but for those who do, the staff members of the national and area Christian education offices stand ready to help.

The superintendent's work as an organizer will often relate to the inauguration of a new program or the organization of a new group within the existing Sunday school. To launch the new program or group successfully, the superintendent will find it helpful to keep several principles in mind:

a. Show the need for the new venture to the greatest possible number of persons who will be affected, directly or indirectly.

b. Give the chance to share in determining its nature and process of realization to the greatest possible number of those essential to the success of the venture.

c. Prepare a well-planned time schedule for the achievement of the new program or group.

d. Assign responsibility for specific tasks contributing to the success of the new venture to the appropriate persons or groups, and secure their acceptance of these assignments.

e. Launch the new venture enthusiastically. Thoroughly publicize the reason for it, the results to be achieved through it, and the need for its support.

5. *A Leader of Worship:* A unified Sunday program of worship and study deserves consideration by our Sunday schools. The increase in teaching time and the elimination of duplication are only two of its many values. For churches with a unified program of worship and study, the church service of worship becomes the worship assembly of the school as well. Any additional worship experience within the school's time is usually in the children's or youth division on a graded basis.

In some Sunday schools the superintendent may be directly responsible for leading worship or may counsel other persons in the leadership of worship. By depending on the pastor or church director of Christian education for help in this field as needed, he or she can become a more competent leader through learning and using the basic principles of public and graded worship.

One of the sections of the church library can provide worship resource materials.

6. *A Personal Counselor:* Any person in an administrative position soon becomes aware that the personal problems of those working within the organization affect their competence. This is as true of Sunday school workers as of others. Many of these problems the superintendent will want to refer to the pastor or some other competent person. In all cases, however, the superintendent will be a better leader if workers feel they can discuss their personal problems as they affect their Sunday school work, knowing that their disclosures will be treated confidentially and with good judgment.

The superintendent should by no means seek to serve as a professional counselor, but a willingness to listen, a strict keeping of confidences, and a genuine Christian concern for discovering avenues of helpfulness will strengthen both leader and staff.

7. *A Symbol:* As the leader of the Sunday school, the superintendent is in many ways a symbol—a symbol of the school. Within the church fellowship as well as in the community and elsewhere, she or he represents the school. Within the school itself the superintendent becomes a symbol to both students and teachers: a symbol of its weakness or of its strength and achievement. The superintendent is identified with the nature and quality of the particular Sunday school within which he or she works.

The Superintendent's Growth

The superintendent who looks at this task and considers the nature of the leadership he or she is called upon to give may well be thankful for not facing the task in one's own strength only. Calling on the pastor, the church as a whole, and co-workers within the Sunday school for support, one is ultimately aware of working together with God in the achievement of Christian education objectives within the lives of the members of the school. If there are times when one doubts an ability to carry out some of these responsibilities, confidence may be renewed by pondering the comment of Paul to the Corinthian church: "But we have this treasure in clay jars, so that it may be made clear that this extraordinary power belongs to God and does not come from us" (2 Corinthians 4:7).

No truly competent superintendent will ever feel completely adequate for all phases of the work. Therefore, he or she will seek constantly to grow both in understanding of the work and in the ability to do it. Some ways to aid this growth are:

1. *Study of Christian Education Magazines and Books:* Magazines published by one's own denomination offer a rich source of help. Some of the articles concern small schools, some concern large schools, but all of them are of value regardless of the size of the school. Some of these articles the superintendent will refer to other workers within the school. It is good, however, to be conversant with their contents.

There are a number of excellent books on Christian education currently available. They differ in quality, of course, and the superintendent will have to decide which to read. The personal recommendation of someone in whom one has confidence, a careful analysis of the descriptive material advertising the new books, or the recognition of a personal need may guide one's choice of specific books. By studying even one carefully chosen book a year, the superintendent will grow measurably in understanding the task and the ways to perform it.

2. *Attendance at Training Schools and Conferences:* Although individual churches do not find it feasible to organize a study course for general superintendents, an increasing number of communities are doing so. Such a class may be organized on a community-wide, state-wide, or even national basis. Area or national conferences for superintendents are usually scheduled by the denominations. Some denominations provide training by correspondence. Conferences with other superintendents, whether informal or as a part of a training school, can bring inspiration as well as information. The effective superintendent will participate in as many such conferences as opportunity and time will permit.

3. *Knowledge of the Curriculum Materials and the Teaching Procedures of Workers:* The superintendent grows not only by increasing a fund of information, but also as one has occasion, testing the workability of this knowledge in connection with the opportunities and problems of the school. As he or she and co-workers make use of their materials or seek together the answers to the problems of their school, the superintendent will grow in leadership stature. This process helps one discover that the authority of helpful guidance is much stronger and more enduring than the authority of position—especially in a volunteer organization such as the Sunday school.

4. *Spiritual Development:* No one stands still spiritually. Any person in a position of spiritual leadership, such as a superintendent, either becomes increasingly conscious of a relationship to God through prayer, work, Bible study, and devotional reading, or strains with futility to maintain the semblance of it. The superin-

tendent must truly be a Christian before becoming an effective administrator, educator, or leader. One's spiritual condition is basic to everything else one is and does. Prayer and Bible study, as an integral part of daily life, will strengthen an awareness of the God whom we serve.

A growing superintendent will find an ever greater thrill in the work and an increasing joy in doing it. This truly important task requires not only the dedication of all that one has but also a willingness to grow and improve.

Chapter 2

The Teaching Ministry of the Sunday School

God calls the church to mission, to share in reconciling to God a separated world and people; to witness to the Good News of God's redeeming love as revealed in the life, death, and resurrection of Jesus Christ.[1]

The church ministers through functions of proclamation, preaching, worship, witness, fellowship, and service; and also in the administration of these functions. Each of the functions is related to the others and at the same time has a special ministry to fulfill in the total mission of the church.

The teaching ministry is designed to undergird all dimensions of the church's mission, even as it in turn is undergirded by the other ministries. It is concerned with the process of teaching and learning, of disciplining the mind, of influencing the development of character through study and instruction, through action and reflection, and with equipping persons for informed participation in mission.

An Effective Sunday School Program

Every thoughtful superintendent will look at the school from time to time with a questioning eye. Seeing adults, young people, and children coming out of their classes at the close of the session, one may feel satisfaction in the fact that they keep coming Sunday after

Sunday. But how much have they benefited? How is the school affecting their lives? The Sunday school is the primary vehicle for the teaching ministry within most local churches. A

An Effective Program Is
Integrated
Graded
Growing
Staffed
Planned

strong and effective program strengthens the entire congregation.

1. *An Integrated Program:* An effective Sunday school program will be an integral part of the total educational effort of the church. In most churches it is the major part. In any case, the Sunday school program will be closely related to the total program of the church. Usually this integration is achieved through a board of Christian education. Such a board is elected by the church to develop and supervise its educational program. The Sunday school superintendent is an ex-officio member of this board and therefore has a part in determining the educational policies of the church, including those which have to do with the Sunday school.

2. *A Graded Curriculum:* An effective Sunday school will have a well-balanced and varied curriculum, graded for the age groups to which the school ministers. The school will be wise to make full use of the curriculum resources and materials provided by its denomination. These materials are based on an intelligent and reverent use of the Bible; they develop a clear understanding of Christian principles; they include evangelistic concern and practice; and they seek to keep the students informed as to the program and mission outreach which their church has through its denomination.

Some churches find that a broadly graded or inter-generational program will best meet their needs. Careful planning can ensure that these types of programs, whether occasional or regular, are appropriate for all the students involved.

3. *A Growing School:* An effective Sunday school will endeavor to increase each year the number of persons enrolled. To say that a school is more interested in quality than in quantity is a poor excuse for not being interested in both. Usually the school that is interested in both quality and quantity does better work in both than the school that emphasizes one to the exclusion of the other.

The Sunday school is an effective evangelistic arm of the church. It provides classes for all ages, infants through senior adults, who meet in small groups where relationships can be built and enjoyed, and an organizational pattern that offers an opportunity for intentional and ongoing visitation.[2]

4. *A Trained Staff:* An effective Sunday school will train, support, and give due recognition to its teachers and officers. The responsibility they carry for encouraging Christian decisions and for guiding growth in the Christian life is somewhat overwhelming, but the rewards are great. To do one's best work, each teacher needs (a) a genuine Christian experience and guidance in growth in it; (b) training and experience in understanding students; (c) a knowledge of the objectives of Christian education; (d) training and experience in using good teaching methods; (e) a sound knowledge of the curriculum materials and resources related to one's teaching responsibility.

5. *Cooperation in Planning:* An effective Sunday school will plan and evaluate its program in the light

of the goals and objectives which have been adopted cooperatively by the board of Christian education and the Sunday school workers, under the leadership of the pastor, the director of Christian education, and the general superintendent.

Effective Christian education programming is the key factor within a congregation that can be associated with helping persons grow in maturity of faith. This conclusion was reached by Search Institute's study of six major Protestant denominations, completed in 1990.[3] The following nine characteristics are descriptive of an effective program of Christian education.

1. The church gives priority to Christian education and understands that it is more than just Sunday school.

2. The pastor is committed, involved, and trained in relation to Christian education.

3. Teachers and leaders are knowledgeable, committed, caring, and teachable.

4. The teaching ministry with adults is given a strong emphasis, and programs for children and youth are offered.

5. The content offered for study addresses biblical understanding, global awareness, moral and value issues, and social issues.

6. A variety of learning activities are used for all age levels.

7. Strong administrative foundations are in place.

8. Parents and guardians are supported in their "teaching" roles.

9. Members are informed, eager, and enthusiastic about the teaching ministry.

A complete description of the planning process and use of an evaluation form is found in chapter 12 of *The*

Teaching Church at Work: A Manual for the Board of Christian Education (Judson Press). After using the evaluation form, the next steps are to establish priorities, write objectives, develop action plans, implement the plans, and evaluate the results. This process becomes a helpful tool for cooperative planning by those responsible for Christian education. The evaluation form, "Characteristics of Effective and Vital Christian Education," is included in Appendix 2 of this book.

The Standard of Achievement, found in Appendix 3, provides another example of goal-setting for Christian education. It was used for many years by one denomination and proved its worth in thousands of churches—small and large, rural and urban. Such a standard, adapted to a local situation, can be referred to continually as a measuring stick by which the work of the school is appraised.

Building an Effective Program

The board of Christian education, with the superintendent as an ex-officio member, is responsible for the educational program of the church. Under its leadership and direction the Sunday school program will be developed. For this purpose the board will enlist

Program Building Calls For
Goals
Analysis
Objectives
Schedule
Responsibility
Informed Membership
Periodic Check-up

the cooperation not only of the superintendent of the Sunday school but also of its teachers and officers. At strategic points, such as the interpretation of curriculum, the changing of time schedules, and the discussion of Sunday school goals and objectives, the church membership may be invited to participate. Such a procedure will bring stability as well as strength to the school because it is done not merely to receive additional ideas and suggestions but also to enlist broad participation in building an effective Sunday school program. Such participation is both an educational experience and a step toward intelligent and enthusiastic support. The judgment and decision of the board of Christian education will determine the extent to which such participation is enlisted. Certainly the staff of the Sunday school can have a large part in the development of the program.

1. *Goals:* In building an effective Sunday school program, the first question concerns goals. What are we trying to accomplish through the total educational program of the church? What is the place of the Sunday school in accomplishing these goals?

Protestant denominations working together in the Cooperative Curriculum Project in 1965 adopted a statement describing an overall goal for a church's teaching ministry. With that as a base, various groups have developed their own statements; the one printed on page 6 is one of them.

Implicit in this statement is the desire for each person to have a personal relationship with God based on God's revelation through Jesus Christ and the Bible as the recorded Word, a faith response to God's love culminating in a commitment to Jesus Christ, participation in the Christian community of the church, and growth in all aspects of personal Christian living.

Christian educators in a local church might well study this statement in the process of determining their own purpose statement for Christian education. The book *The Teaching Church at Work: A Manual for the*

Board of Christian Education includes a workshop designed to assist a local church in this process. Another workshop, "Biblical Foundations for Christian Education," could also be helpful in providing background for a church's educational ministry. It is listed in "Collection" and may be obtained from area or national denominational offices.

This overall goal, with consideration of appropriate aspects for various age levels, applies to the total Christian fellowship of the church in worship, study, service, and witness. Some portions of it are realized through the Sunday worship services of the church, some through the various group meetings held during the week. Others are achieved most effectively through the Sunday school.

This study of a Christian education goal will result in four improvements:

a. A clarification of the goal of the Sunday school.

b. A better understanding of the relationship between the Sunday school and other organized phases of church life.

c. A delegation of responsibility to the various groups functioning in church life, such as evening youth fellowship groups, men's and women's organizations, and especially, the Sunday school.

d. The elimination of irrelevant or harmful customs and the strengthening of practices which promote the goal of the school.

2. *Analysis:* When a thorough study has been made of the goal of Christian education and of the responsibilities of the Sunday school toward its realization, the next step involves an analysis of the present school activities and program for children, youth, and adults:

a. What age groups are we serving through our Sunday school?

b. How many persons are reached in each age group?

c. How effective are these age groups (classes or departments) in achieving the desired goals and objectives of the Sunday school in the lives of their members?

d. Which activities or program elements should be eliminated? What should be strengthened? What should be added?

An evaluation form, "Characteristics of Effective and Vital Christian Education," focuses on the characteristics reached as a conclusion in the Search Institute's study of effective Christian education. (This form may be found in Appendix 2.) When the evaluation form is completed by many persons of all ages within a congregation, it provides an opportunity to analyze areas of strength and those needing improvement in the current Christian education program.

3. *Specific Objectives:* Clear objectives, following a thorough analysis of the present program, constitute the groundwork for building an effective program. These matters must be studied carefully if that which is built on them is to be a sound program. Next, plan the specific steps by which the improved program will be achieved. Assign responsibility for each step. Although this can be done at any time, an especially good time is the spring or late summer. Out of such a planning session can come long-range plans, as well as specific objectives for the coming year.

In planning specific steps for the immediate present and for the long-term future, answers to the following questions can prove helpful.

a. In the light of the general goals and of our present program, what are our most urgent needs?

b. What specific objectives grow out of these needs?

c. When can these objectives be realized?

d. Who is responsible for the fulfillment of each specific objective?

e. What resources are available?

f. How can we keep our church and community informed as to our objectives and achievements?

The following comments refer to the questions, in turn.

The more urgent needs, on investigation, may be found to relate to the curriculum, the teachers, the training of leaders, the equipment and room arrangement, the outreach to new students, or the relationship of the Sunday school to other parts of the church program.

Some of these needs can be met easily and quickly. These can be assigned to the appropriate persons for attention within a specified time. From the remaining suggestions, choose those that seem the more urgent.

At this point the group will proceed with wisdom and faith—wisdom in choosing objectives possible of achievement and faith in selecting objectives that will require dedicated time, ability, and energy to achieve. Furthermore, these objectives will be specific. How much of an increase in enrollment, for example, will be sought during the next year and how shall it be obtained? How shall regularity of attendance be promoted? What new classes need to be set up if the school is to minister to all ages effectively? Does any class need to be shifted to a different room to provide more adequate space for all? What kinds of leadership training will be organized? How many present and prospective teachers will we strive to enlist in these training classes? The answers to these and other questions will be expressed in the objectives adopted.

4. *Schedule:* By what date are these objectives to be achieved? A four- or five-year program of development, expressed in long-term goals, is a valuable guide for any Sunday school. Every school, however, will do well to set up some objectives on an annual basis. These may be complete in themselves or they may be steps in the achievement of a comprehensive five-year goal.

In this connection, examine the Sunday school calendar for the year and note its principal dates. Integrate the schedule for the achievement of these objectives with the continuing calendar of the school. A change of classrooms, for example, might take place in September or October, while a leadership school might be held in October-November or January-February. If a leadership class for training prospective workers is held during the morning Sunday school session, it can be held during those months when special all-school programs will not interfere with it.

5. *Responsibility:* Assigning responsibility is an important step in fulfilling any objective. Certain persons, by virtue of their committee or staff designations, automatically become responsible for certain objectives. Even so, secure their consent to assume any specific assignments as part of their continuing work.

It is equally important to give due recognition to those who have carried responsibility to successful completion. To assign responsibility, to secure consent, to recognize achievement—these are three important steps in stimulating full personal effort.

Fortunately, no church has to meet its Christian teaching needs without help. In addition to those resources which every church has within itself or within its community, denominational offices, area or national, frequently can be of assistance.

6. *Inform*: It is important that the Sunday school keep both the church and the community informed as to its objectives and achievements. Such publicity makes it easier to enlist additional persons in the program, and it inspires those already sharing in it to participate more wholeheartedly.

The best form of publicity, of course, is the contagious enthusiasm of those who feel that they are participating in a worthy teaching program. In addition, the objectives, achievements, and values of the Sunday school can be continuously brought to the attention of the potential constituency. A special annual event provides an excellent opportunity to do this, but it can be supplemented through more frequent publicity. The weekly or monthly church paper, if the church has one, provides space in which the activities and progress of the school may be noted. From time to time, when the occasion merits it, letters to the constituency will inform them concerning some major event. Enlist the cooperation of the pastor in keeping the work of the school before the members of the church. Newspapers will print newsworthy items. These will keep the community aware of the value of the Sunday school and will strengthen the conviction of those sharing in the school that they are part of a significant organization.

7. *Check-up:* It is not wise to wait until near the end of the year to see how well the year's objectives are being achieved. More frequent check-up is advisable. A brief monthly review of objectives and results to date presents an opportunity to remedy laxity and to encourage school progress.

An annual "achievement day" might be the occasion when objectives of the past year are reviewed and the successes and failures are noted. Such an emphasis serves as a spur to achievement and as a stimulus to morale, provided that the objectives are a true challenge and the successes are noteworthy. The fall Rally Day or Christian Education Week might serve the purpose of such an "achievement day." In any case, the whole church would be informed of both the objectives and the results attained.

Teaching Materials

As previously stated, the teaching experience in its most elementary form involves three things: students, teacher, and that which is taught and learned. The materials, therefore, that the teacher uses as an aid to teaching and those the student uses as an aid to learning are of strategic importance. These will help the Sunday school move to-

Effective Teaching Materials Will Be
Biblical
Denominational
Evangelistic
Mission-focused
Graded

ward accomplishing its basic tasks of reaching and teaching people, winning people to Jesus Christ and the church, discipling, and ministering to and with people.[4] The following five criteria of effective teaching materials enlarge upon these tasks.

1. *Biblical:* The Bible is basic to our teaching. All teaching materials, therefore, will display a reverent use of the Bible and an intelligent understanding of its message and central worth.

Over a period of years the entire biblical message will be the focus of systematic study. Students at each age level, as well as their teachers, will have hands-on experiences in using the Bible. Persons will have opportunities to share faith experiences with one another and encourage an understanding and application of the Bible's message.

2. *Denominational:* Through the curriculum or the use of timely and age-appropriate supplemental materials, students will be informed of the distinctive principles for which their denomination stands: they will be aware of the nature and extent of their worldwide mission.

3. *Evangelistic:* The focus on a decision for Christ as Lord and Savior, responsible participation in the life of the church, and a full Christian witness in vocational and community life can be the experience of every person of accountable age enlisted in the school. Such a purpose will motivate the school's teaching program when it permeates all of the teaching materials used in the school. Classes and group studies can provide opportunities for persons to establish relationships, share faith experiences, maintain contact and pray for one another in the process of decision making.

4. *Mission-focused:* A strong mission program at home and abroad is imperative. Such mission effort can be maintained and extended only as church members are inspired by a clear understanding of the program. Effective curriculum materials can aid the teacher in developing the mission consciousness of the students not only through knowledge but also by stimulating cooperative action projects that demonstrate a caring concern in local, national, and international settings.

5. *Graded:* The experience of growth is God-given. Persons are constantly changing in their interests and understanding from infancy through adulthood. Classes in the Sunday school respond to the needs of students at each age level through the use of appropriate curriculum resources for various groupings of stu-

dents. In some churches, working with a combined group of kindergarten and first-grade students (essentially nonreaders) has proved helpful. Where a middle school is part of the local public education system, a similar grouping may be appropriate in the church school.

Effective curriculum and class structure can offer an environment for growing Christians to observe faith in action, to put Bible truths to work in a safe setting, and to face the challenges of new forms of service and ministry among supportive, caring persons.

Three types of teaching materials are available for churches; namely, graded, uniform, and elective.

Graded resources embody effective methods of teaching which are graduated to the age level, understanding, and experience of the student. The needs and interests of the student are brought to the Bible in order that the light of the Word of God may shine upon them. The way is opened for personal response through a variety of learning experiences, practical activities, and day-by-day living.

Uniform resources start each lesson with a portion of Scripture, which is then applied to life in terms of the needs of varying groups. Persons at all age levels are studying at least portions of the same Bible passage on any given Sunday.

Elective resources are provided for the purpose of exploring a chosen subject or as an occasional change from other teaching resources. Some churches may find that an intergenerational class or a family cluster learning group provides stimulation for learning. A broadly graded class, such as one in which grades one through six meet together, may prove helpful for situations where there are few students of any one grade.

If special questions arise—possibly at the point of grading classes, selecting curriculum, or in helping teachers make the best use of teaching materials—the superintendent can get in touch with Christian education leaders in the denominational office.

Location, Rooms, and Equipment

Sunday school groups or classes will usually meet in the church building. In some circumstances they may meet in other locations such as homes, community buildings, or on some occasions, a retreat center. It is the responsibility of the congregation to furnish facilities appropriate for study which will foster the attitude that "important learning happens here." Children, youth, and adults alike are affected by the setting in which the teaching takes place. Provide them with surroundings that are conducive to learning.

Every church, no matter how large or how small, can improve its teaching program by keeping its rooms clean, well lighted, correctly ventilated, and adequately equipped. For personal safety, provide windows in the doors of individual classrooms. Cheerful but restful colors materially affect both teachers and students. Dirt and disorder make doubly oppressive an already cramped space; whereas a room that is clean, with floors, chairs, and woodwork dusted, and with walls and ceiling free from cobwebs, becomes an invitation to better teaching and learning. It is best to have sturdy and comfortable chairs, correctly graded as to size for the age group that will be using them. Large cushions or carpeted areas may also be used effectively.

The problem of space is frequently a serious one, caused by either too much or too little space. Use movable partitions to divide a large room for use by several groups or to provide a cozier atmosphere for a few people meeting in a large space. Partitions may be purchased or constructed by members of the congregation. Some have found portable storage cabinets useful as room dividers.

Too little space sometimes requires schedule shifts to enable maximum participation for all. The superintendent or another trained leader can assist teachers to make the best use of the space that is available. No matter how inadequate classroom space may be, keep it clean, cheerful, and well ventilated.

When class areas serve multiple purposes or are used by outside groups during the week, communication and cooperation are essential. A clear understanding of responsibilities is important in maintaining an attractive meeting place for all.

Special equipment is being added by many churches because excellent audiovisual teaching materials are now available to strengthen the teaching program of the church. A combination filmstrip and slide projector, cassette tape player, or an overhead projector may be used to advantage with all age groups when their use also involves interaction among class members. No audiovisual resource is a substitute for careful preparation by the teacher. Judicious use of nonprojected visuals (pictures, charts, maps, posters), placed at student eye level, strengthens the teaching/learning process.

With the increased number of high-quality religious films, a motion picture projector and a VCR (videocassette recorder) are good investments for many churches. Their initial cost, plus the cost of film or video rentals, may make them seem quite expensive. In such situations, however, a group of churches, through a council of churches or on their own initiative, may desire to purchase such equipment cooperatively.

Using a slide or movie camera or a portable camcorder, a class of students can plan and create their own films or videos. Members of the congregation who have this equipment may be willing to assist class groups wishing to take advantage of these resources. Sharing the results of this creative learning experience can enrich other groups, the whole Sunday school, or the congregation.

The Church Library

A church library can be a valuable asset to the Sunday school. It requires an accessible space, adequate shelves for the attractive display of books and magazines, and an enthusiastic librarian who will not only catalog the books properly but will also promote the use of the library.

The nature of the library will be determined by the use which the church plans to make of it. There are three broad classifications, any one or all of which may be served by the library: books for Sunday school workers; religious books for parents and children to use in the home; books of general interest to the church membership.

Most churches begin with a library for Sunday school workers, or at least include books for such workers. An item in the Christian education budget can make possible a reasonable number of additions to the library each year. Suggestions for such additions may be found in the denomination's catalog or by writing to the Christian education department of the denomination.

Equally important is the goal of getting workers to use the library. This can be done through recommending specific books to those persons who will find them helpful. Publicizing recent additions to the library with an explanation of the appeal that led to their choice and calling attention to two or three relevant books at each meeting of teachers are additional ways of stimulating interest in the library. Do not neglect the library as a valuable means of training teachers!

Chapter 3

Organizing and Administering the Sunday School

Christian teaching, in some form or other, has been a function of the Christian church from its inception. The Sunday school as we know it today, however, is of more recent origin. It has evolved from an eighteenth-century experiment by a devout Christian layman, Robert Raikes, in teaching boys and girls to read and write. These schools, organized first in England, were designed to help the children who worked long hours in factories on every weekday; hence, they met on Sunday, and for educational materials they used chiefly the Bible.

These Sunday schools later broadened their program to include religious training for youth and adults. They were held in church buildings and usually drew upon the members of the church for their teachers and officers. They functioned, however, as separate organizations. Each had administrative autonomy and raised its own budget. From time to time the school made a contribution to the church in return for the use of its facilities. As these Sunday schools grew, they provided many laypersons with an opportunity for Christian service and leadership. As a result of the intimate and informal fellowship in study and teaching they provided, they won the devotion of millions.

During the first half of the twentieth century, it was

perceived that the teaching responsibility of the church and the purpose of the Sunday school were identical, and there has been a significant effort to make the Sunday school an integral part of the church organization and program. This awakened understanding that Christian teaching is the responsibility of the whole church is revealed in the use of such designations as "the school of the church," "the church school," and "the Sunday church school."

The Sunday school, therefore, is the whole church, as a church, communicating the gospel to children, youth, and adults through the teaching process. This is the concern of the whole church and is to be achieved through all its program. The Sunday school, the largest organization for Christian education in the church, is an expression of this purpose. Administratively, therefore, the Sunday school will be accountable to the church, and the church will be responsible for the effective ministry of the Sunday school. It is understood, of course, that the church seeks to expand its educational program beyond the Sunday school to include the vacation church school, the weekday church school, the school of missions, and other Christian education activities.

The true strength of the Sunday school lies in its enlistment of our finest laypersons in the teaching program of the church. The contagion of their dedicated lives and devoted spirit gives power to the Christian truth they seek to communicate. The Sunday school enables them to share their faith. This they do through who they are and through the help which they give to others.

How Will the School Be Organized?

The organization of the Sunday school involves two phases: its relationship to the church as a whole and its organization within itself.

The Church at Study: The Sunday school is the church at study on Sunday morning. It will be administered, therefore, by the church through its board of Christian education. The general superintendent, as the executive charged with the administration of the school, is an ex-officio member of the board of Christian education. As such, the superintendent shares in making all board decisions.

The board of Christian education is responsible for the appointment of all Sunday school officers and teachers serving under the general superintendent.

The board of Christian education is responsible for organizing leader development opportunities for the Sunday school staff, and it is expected to enlist new personnel for the leadership of the educational program.

The board of Christian education, through its age-group committees (children, youth, and adult), is concerned with discovering new ways of strengthening the church's educational program within these three age divisions.

The board of Christian education will bring other special resources to the Sunday school through such committees as those for mission and stewardship education, leader development, music, drama, worship, recreation, camping, and audiovisual aids.

Because of administrative responsibilities, the superintendent of the school will serve not only as an ex-officio member of the board of Christian education, but may also be an ex-officio member of its subcommittees. The superintendent, concerned with the general excellence of the school and probably the person best informed as to its total needs, will prove to be a key member in the work of the board as it relates to the Sunday school.

The Sunday School Pattern: Elements describing the educational structure recommended for the Sunday school are as follows:[5]

1. a statement of the *purpose*, or a description of the *primary* contribution the Sunday school makes to the church's overall mission;

2. the *constituency* of the Sunday school, i.e., those persons for whose sake the church school is designed and administered;

3. the *grouping of persons* for teaching-learning in the Sunday school;

4. the *frequency* with which groups meet for learning experiences;

5. the *time span for each meeting* or gathering of the teaching-learning groups;

6. the *leaders* required for operating the Sunday school;

7. the *administration* of the Sunday school.

Each of these elements influences the others and each is but one part of a total dynamic educational construct. The decisions made about each element serve as a guide to persons who want to provide Christian education opportunities by using the setting the "Sunday school." Below, each element is discussed in turn.

1. The Primary Contribution of the Sunday School

The primary contribution of the Sunday school to the whole of the church's educational ministry is its focus upon and use of the disciplines and structures of a *school*. The Sunday school offers persons, of whatever age, opportunities to engage in a regularly scheduled, year-round learning effort to understand and appropriate the meanings and experiences of the Christian faith and life. The Sunday school program can help persons interrelate a wide range of issues, concerns, and responsibilities in light of: (a) an understanding of the Bible, and (b) the insights of a Christian tradition that holds these concerns and responsibilities to be a primary means by which God's truth is revealed.

Involvement in church school experiences is a systematic way by which persons can relate their persistent life concerns to the meaning and experiences of the gospel. It can also give them continuing guidance in living the Christian faith in the world as they grow in their awareness of God revealed in Jesus Christ, and as they respond to God in faith and love.

2. Constituency of the Sunday School

The Sunday school is for persons of all ages. It includes both those who have responded to the call of Christ as his disciples and those who are inquiring into the meaning of the Christian gospel but who have not yet committed themselves to it. Such an inclusive membership means that the Sunday school will probably involve the largest number of learners of all settings in a church's educational ministry.

At the beginning of the Sunday school year, persons may be asked to register for courses of study to be offered by the school that particular year. It should be made clear to the registrant (or to parents or guardian) that the school is designed for those who want to discover the meaning of the Christian gospel at the level of inquiry appropriate to their age. The act of registering will remind persons of the learning purpose of the school. After the beginning of the school year it will be helpful to provide for the enrollment and orientation of persons to the teaching-learning units already in process.

3. Grouping in the Sunday School

Appropriate grouping within the Sunday school will be flexible and adaptable to:

the total number of students;

the ability, nature, and maturation of the students;

the commonalities of interests of persons who are potential members of learning groups; and

the training and experiences of the teachers or teaching teams.

Church school administrators will plan for each group to continue in existence only long enough to achieve its intended learnings, recognizing that too frequent re-grouping can detract from the learning experience while remaining over-long in one group can stultify it, particularly for youth and adults. Every group, regardless of its length of existence, provides for maximum personal involvement.

The Sunday school is frequently organized on a two-grade basis (2- and 3-year-olds, 4- and 5-year-olds, grades 1 and 2, and so forth). Curriculum resources developed for this plan can also be used in Sunday schools operating on a one- or three-grade basis and generally contain directions for adaptation.

In some congregations local factors may call for grouping by a single grade or age or by as many as three grades or ages. It is good to recognize that a class of one or two students can be effective in Christian teaching. The skillful teacher of such a class will capitalize on these advantages: developing personal relationships; meeting individual needs; easier communication; trying new or different activities; and ease in shifting learning locations.

Factors other than school grade, pre-elementary age, or post-school age may also be used as bases for grouping persons in the Sunday school. These factors include the learners' interests, concerns, talents and abilities, growth, maturation, previous experiences, types of commitment, exceptional physical or mental capacities. Whatever the basis for grouping, the need for continuous teaching-learning of the Christian faith in groups goes on throughout life. The Sunday school is designed to meet this need for all groups of all ages however related to the congregation.

The Sunday school may use a variety of groupings: classes of learners, departments (groupings of classes), the total school, family or residential groups, teachers or leaders of classes, administrators and supervisors, and teachers and administrators. In the last three of these classifications, the ones dealing with Sunday school leaders, the persons will sometimes be grouped as teachers or leaders of classes for the purpose of sharing common concerns and problems. Administrators and supervisors may come together at designated times to consider specific issues in their work. On occasion, Sunday school teachers and administrators will form a single group to consider problems of concern to both.

4. Frequency of Gatherings in the Sunday School

While provision should be made for flexibility and adaptation, the curriculum plan proposes the following frequency of gatherings:

a. Classes for learners in the Sunday school will meet at designated times once a week on a year-round basis, probably on Sunday morning. However, there is a growing trend for classes in the Sunday school to meet at times other than or in addition to Sunday morning.

b. Classes for potential new leaders in the Sunday school and also for persons who have had teaching experience and who wish to reenter the Sunday school faculty may meet at designated times once a week on a year-round basis or as appropriate.

c. Groups of classes or the total school may meet for special purposes, though these meetings will probably be infrequent ones.

d. Leaders will have special meetings for training events supporting the Sunday school.

5. Time Span of Gatherings in the Sunday School

It is essential that persons in any learning group have sufficient time for significant interchange, communication, and the development of relationships. In general, most graded resources have been designed to provide teaching-learning experiences based upon a time span of 45 to 60 minutes. Recognizing that longer sessions, under competent teachers, will contribute to more meaningful learning experiences, some churches may elect to expand their teaching time for children to 75 to 90 minutes. In many curriculum resources there is sufficient or additional material for expanding the teaching time.

The length of time required for producing changes in understandings, attitudes, and action patterns will vary from church to church and from group to group. However, it is assumed that there are minimal time limits below which fruitful teaching-learning experiences are not likely to occur, just as there are terminal points beyond which teachers and pupils experience diminishing returns in learning for the time invested.

The longer periods for teaching-learning sessions

using the optional or supplementary teaching resources in the graded Sunday school curriculum materials for children in the church school can provide the opportunity for quality education for pupils at every age level and allow time for necessary maintenance tasks (such as taking attendance, making announcements, and creating a climate of friendliness and concern). The longer sessions also permit the entire school, or parts of it, to meet on special occasions to celebrate great events in the life of the church or to share with one another some common themes and emphases within the teaching-learning units. In other situations the additional session time may be used for field trips and special study projects related to the congregation's educational ministry.

Children, perhaps more than youth and adults, are affected negatively by pressure, which often results when insufficient time is allowed for learning experiences in their Sunday school groups. For this reason an increasing number of churches have moved the Sunday school sessions for children to a weekday or Saturday, where they may have an uninterrupted period of two or two-and-one-half hours. Most churches, however, continue to feel that Sunday morning provides their best opportunity to reach the greatest number of children, and many have established an expanded session time for their learning. Usually, this "expanded" period is two hours or more long and covers both the time set for adult classes and for the morning worship services of the church. The expanded session is a single, unified session, with a *single* purpose and all activities, including worship, planned to contribute to that purpose.

When such an expansion of teaching time is not immediately possible, a church may elect to provide a relaxed class atmosphere for whatever class time is available. To do this they may extend the use of the curriculum teaching materials provided for one session to cover two or more sessions. This will mean ignoring weekly dates that may be on the curriculum and adjusting the order in which materials are used so that emphases for special days (Christmas, Easter, and so forth) come at the appropriate times. It will also allow teachers to take advantage of some of the optional activities included in the curriculum and to have an unhurried and therefore greater depth of relationship with the class members.

6. Leadership in the Sunday School

Designated leaders in the Sunday school include those who teach, those who supervise and administer (such as superintendents and other officers), and those who are called on for special resources (music, art, drama, etc.). The minister(s) of the congregation (pastor, minister of Christian education, and other associate ministers) is/are seen as the ones carrying primary responsibility for leading and teaching the other designated leaders of the Sunday school. The minister(s) is the congregation's chief theological resource person and is the teacher of Sunday school leaders.

Leaders or teachers with special skills and abilities may be commissioned to help other teachers improve the quality and effectiveness of their teaching by assisting the pastor in giving leadership to events and meetings related to these concerns. In addition, resource persons from the community or beyond may from time to time lead in the various training events for leaders.

The congregation has a responsibility to minister to the persons selected for designated leadership in its Sunday school. This ministry should touch their personal faith as well as their assigned teaching tasks. Most often this ministry to Sunday school leaders will take place within the local congregation; sometimes there will be leader development events sponsored by two or more churches within a given geographical area. It is expected that all designated leaders in the Sunday school will receive training before their appointment and during their time of service.

7. The Administration of the Sunday School

The administration of the Sunday school is the responsibility of persons commissioned for this task by the congregation. Generally Sunday school administration will be a part of the work directed by a congregation's board or committee of Christian education, including the Sunday school superintendent. All learning groups within the church will operate within the policies set by this administrative committee or board.

The general superintendent is the person responsible for the Sunday school. All matters concerned with the effective functioning of the school, including those whose ultimate decision resides with the board of Christian education, should clear through the general superintendent. On the board of Christian education may be coordinators of ministry with children, youth, and adults. These persons will work closely with the age-group personnel in the various departments. In case of any serious difference of opinion between an age-group coordinator and the Sunday school superintendent, the board of Christian education is the arbiter. Ordinarily, however, such arbitration is not necessary because all the board members as well as the superintendent are interested in a strong Christian teaching program for the church.

A Sunday school of average size requires, in addition

to the general superintendent and the departmental officers and teachers previously mentioned, one or more assistant superintendents, a secretary, and possibly a treasurer.

The number of assistant superintendents depends upon the number of functions assigned to them. At least have one assistant superintendent in training as a potential successor to the present superintendent. Whether or not the church is following the wise system of rotation in office through a mandatory limit on the number of successive years a person may serve in one office, it is always advisable that others be in training for responsible leadership.

Much of the secret of any superintendent's success lies in the intelligent distribution of responsibility. In a small school the superintendent and one assistant, together with teachers and the board of Christian education, can easily handle the varied activities of the school. But even so, the superintendent ought to let an assistant and other staff members grow through giving them increased responsibility. The test of the administrative ability of a superintendent in a school of any size is not one's ability to do everything alone but enabling others to use their talents in doing the work.

One word of caution: the number of administrative personnel should be limited to those essential to the efficient functioning of the school. It is time to simplify when the administrative machinery takes more energy to keep it running than to do the job.

The Superintendent's Use of Records

Most superintendents are familiar with curriculum resources available to the Sunday schools. Some may not be so fully aware of the administrative helps also available.

Records are of many types and serve various ends. No record need be kept, however, unless it fulfills a purpose that is clearly understood and considered important.

Attendance records have both group and individual values. The attendance within a department or in the whole school shows, over a period of time, whether or not the school is growing in the number of persons it is reaching. But records also show the regularity of attendance for individual students and indicate those who have dropped out or been lost otherwise to the school. In addition, records will show class, departmental, and total school attendance. An analysis of these figures and a search for the reasons why certain classes or departments show more regularity of attendance than others will do much to reveal the points of strength and weakness within the school's program, teaching staff, and family interest.

Most schools need more adequate records of each individual's progress within the educational program of the church and its school. Such a record would give the date when the student became a member of the school, progress through the classes and departments, regularity of attendance, special achievements, and personal development in leadership ability and experience.

Special records on the leadership of the school may also prove valuable. Such records indicate any courses of study taken by each officer and teacher, regularity of attendance at teachers' meetings, and other leadership information considered desirable.

The kind of financial records to be kept depends on

the extent to which the Sunday school is integrated into the financial structure of the church as a whole. The financial records of a school which is a separate organization underwriting its own budget will be different from those of a school whose expenses are included in the budget of the church.

Enlisting and Training Teachers

Leaders with different responsibilities are essential to the educational program of the Sunday school. Of all the leaders, none is more needed than a good teacher. The small church with only a few classes is as much in need of good teachers as is the largest Sunday school. Finding such teachers is one of the responsibilities of the board of Christian education. When choosing teachers, certain factors need to be borne in mind.

Conviction: The church must impress upon all its members that Christian education is important to its life and that its program of Christian education, therefore, should be the finest possible. This conviction can be created and continuously strengthened through the pastor's sermons, through items in the church paper, through adequate equipment and financial support for the school's program, and through special ceremonies that keep Christian education and its workers prominent in the thinking of church members. Among the last named are installation services, an annual commissioning of officers and teachers, the annual banquet for Sunday school workers, and the annual conference to plan the educational program of the church.

When the board of Christian education is considering the name of a prospective teacher, how should it proceed? (a) Be sure, through careful investigation and consideration that the person is the one wanted for that particular teaching opportunity. (b) Choose carefully the right person to approach a prospective teacher with the invitation to teach. This may be a department superintendent, the pastor, the church director, the superintendent, or some member of the board of Christian education. It may seem wise to send two persons to extend the invitation to serve. Whoever is sent should be recognized as speaking for the board of Christian education and the church as a whole. (c) Arrange a personal conference in which there is time to present adequately the challenge of the new responsibility. A casual call on the telephone or a quick urging during the rush between Sunday services may make the invitation seem trivial. Since teaching is important, do not pretend that it is an easy task; rather, emphasize the great possibilities it affords to influence others for Christ and the conviction of the board of Christian education that the person approached is big enough for the job. (d) Those persons who sincerely doubt their ability to teach or lead may begin their service as apprentice teachers or associate teachers.

It is important for the superintendent to see that the work of the Sunday school is constantly publicized. A continuous stream of news of specific educational undertakings and achievements provides better publicity than general statements to the effect that Christian education is important.

Stewardship: The church must develop among its members a sense of responsibility for the Christian stewardship of time and ability, as well as of money. New members, as they are welcomed into the Sunday school, can be led to recognize this responsibility and make personal commitments in the light of it. The church, of course, is also responsible for distributing tasks and opportunities for service in such fashion that many persons can share in the work.

In addition to the basic policies that influence, consciously or otherwise, the procuring of teachers, there are certain procedures that can help in discovering prospective teachers: (a) Study the church membership roll and consider the possibilities of each member. (b) Ask teachers of older youth and adult classes to suggest the names of those within their classes who might make good teachers. (c) Consider persons within the women's or men's organizations who have potential or actual leadership ability in relation to the needs of the school. (d) Take note of those who are teaching in the local public schools or colleges. (e) Hold a personal conference with each new church member to discover future prospective teachers. (f) Attempt to enlist persons for service through individual conferences and through conferences with small groups or classes.

Abusive Relationships: The protection of children is a primary motivation for the congregation that desires to establish policies to prevent child abuse within the church.[6] The whole church must be aware of what is considered abuse and know what to do about it. It is very important for the governing board of the church to develop and adopt a policy to prevent abuse. Public schools are encouraged to perform background checks; churches can do this also for every individual who works with children or youth, both paid professionals and volunteers. Other actions that can help to safeguard the lives of children and youth from abusive teachers and leaders include:

• Screen persons who want to work with minors in the church. Interview them personally, asking specific background questions and why they want to work with children.

• Do not be afraid to refuse to allow someone to work with children. Find some other function in the church that does not involve direct contact with children, or place the person in a highly supervised position.

• Set rules for accountability. Require that two adults be present at all times; that persons be active in the church for six months before working with minors.

• Supervise workers, making regular and unannounced visits to every classroom and program. Provide windows in classroom doors or leave them open.

Training: Teachers need to acquire information and to develop teaching skills; they also need inspiration and encouragement in their work. They usually feel the need for training in biblical knowledge. They need to be informed about the characteristics of the students they teach. Through training, a good teacher will become acquainted with the values inherent in various methods of teaching, especially those suited for use with a particular grade level. Any teacher who has discovered the relationship of the class to the total program of the church will benefit personally and will be a better teacher. Training will help a teacher to understand the various areas of curriculum interest and their meaning for the students.

Leader development may be classified as formal and informal. Formal leadership education refers to specific courses of study carried on under supervision. Most denominations provide leader training resources for use in local churches. On many occasions denominations or ecumenical groups provide workshops for Sunday school teachers in a given geographic area.

Included usually are courses on the Bible, personal Christian living, characteristics of students, and methods of teaching. There are specialized workshops for workers with children, with youth, and with adults, as well as for superintendents and others who carry administrative responsibilities. Contact your denominational office for assistance in training teachers.

One denomination has published *Collection*, a description of eighty workshops designed for use in the local church, to be led by an experienced pastor or lay leader. Most are for a two-hour presentation. Each workshop contains a purpose statement, description of suggested settings, instructions for the leader, a list of resources needed, an outline, and step-by-step plans. These workshops are available through regional or national denominational offices for a small fee.

Informal leadership training refers to (a) apprentice teaching, (b) practice teaching under supervision, (c) observing other teachers, (d) monthly teachers' meetings, (e) conferences with leaders from other Sunday schools at community, state, or national gatherings, (f) guided reading of books and magazines.

A certificate or some other worthy method of recognizing a person's progress in a balanced program of training through personal religious development, discipleship, and educational growth will be rewarding.

The church that values leadership qualities will want to consider the following criteria.

General characteristics of church leaders

is committed to Jesus Christ
helps a group establish a climate of trust,
     openness, frankness

gives time and energy to train for a leadership
task

helps a group set its own goals and organize to
reach its goals

sees the potential in others

attends worship services and church activities

is willing to accept and use other persons' points
of view

has high regard for oneself and is able to assess
own strengths and limitations

acts out of Christian commitment in all avenues
of life.

Specific qualities for educational leaders

gives information in an interesting way

has a deep respect for the Bible

involves the group in making decisions about its
life and study

plans sessions well ahead and has materials
ready

is able to express own beliefs

understands how persons learn

helps members of the group to learn from their
own experiences

is willing to use recommended materials

knows how to listen to others.[7]

Genuine growth in Christian leadership comes, of
course, not merely from training, but primarily from a
deep sense of one's Christian stewardship of time and
ability, coupled with a willingness to undertake tasks
that may seem to be beyond one's powers. Such a willingness is nurtured and stimulated through the faith
that one is working with God. Basic to any training,
therefore, will be the daily practice of prayer, devotional

reading, and meditation. The pressure of accumulating tasks must never be permitted to crowd these practices from the daily schedule of the Christian worker.

Chapter 4

The General Superintendent Works with Others

As the general superintendent goes about the work, he or she will find that many people contribute to the effectiveness of administrative leadership. In fact, not only one's satisfaction in the task but also the morale of the school will be affected greatly by those with whom the superintendent is associated. Working relationships with them, therefore, are important. Through them the work of the school gets done; through them the Christian teaching program of the school achieves its goals.

Valuable Relationships

1. *The Students:* In one sense, the superintendent works with all the members of the Sunday school classes. But many relationships with them are indirect; that is, through the teachers and administrative staff. Yet in the course of a year there will be many occasions to be in direct personal contact with the students. To them the superintendent is the symbol of the Sunday school. Such identification

The Superintendent Works With
Students
Parents
Teachers
Minister
Director of Christian Education
Board of Christian Education
Church and Community
The Administrative Staff

brings opportunities as well as responsibilities. A superintendent who knows the name of each person in the school, speaks with each one directly, and makes occasional visits to each classroom can establish a valuable rapport with students of all ages. The youth who today admires the superintendent and the spirit in which the work is done may be inspired, ten years from now, to accept the same honor and responsibility. Any superintendent with a long-term concern for the growth and improvement of the school will not neglect relationships with the students—children and youth, as well as adults.

2. *The Parents:* The family plays a vital role in the faith development and nurture of young people. Recent studies have shown that much will be gained by including parents in the process of planning for church-related programs for children and youth.[8] Communication, cooperation, and feelings of ownership are the likely result from involving parents when Christian education decisions are being made. The superintendent who recognizes the value of relationships with parents will find ways to utilize personal contacts, letters, and church newsletters. Invite parents' participation and support in the learning process through suggested activities at home as well as in the Sunday school.

3. *The Teachers:* No matter how large or small a school may be, teachers are essential members of the Sunday school staff, and the superintendent must work with them. If teachers enjoy their work, if they have the equipment they need, if they are encouraged in their search for added training, and if they feel that their achievements are sincerely appreciated and rec-

ognized, they will produce amazing results with their students.

The superintendent of a small school usually is in close contact with teachers. Together they work and plan in order that their school may grow and improve its program. In a larger school, the normal channels of communication between the general superintendent and the teachers are through the departmental superintendents. But whatever the size of the school, the relationship between the superintendent and the teachers is of vital importance.

The devotion of the superintendent to the task becomes an inspiration to the teachers. If they feel genuine appreciation of the importance of this responsibility, they will respond more readily to any challenge to them to do their work well. The authority of the superintendent is most effectively wielded through encouragement, persuasion, and the power of example. The teachers work for the same reasons that a superintendent does: loyalty to Christ and the church, genuine interest in persons, and a conviction that the teaching ministry of the church is important. The superintendent's leadership will be successful to the extent that co-workers are persuaded that when suggestions are made they will bring improvement to the Sunday school.

The superintendent, as an ex-officio member of the board of Christian education, has a voice in the choice of teachers, but the relationship to them does not stop there. Through personal comments and guidance a superintendent helps teachers to recognize and appreciate the significance of their opportunities, encouraging each teacher to increase leadership skills through recommended reading and study, through participation in conferences, and through attendance at training classes. It is helpful to show an understanding of each teacher's work, commenting with approval upon noteworthy achievements and calling attention to possible changes that will make for improvement. This will be based in part on annual (if not more frequent) visits to the classroom while the class is in session, as well as other observations. Growth through Christian training and experience can be as real for teachers as for students. The superintendent can help to make it so.

4. *The Minister:* The minister is the administrative leader of the church as a whole, as the superintendent is the administrative leader of the Sunday school, a part of that whole. Other relationships, of course, exist between them: the minister is the pastor of the church and the superintendent is one of the members; the minister is the worship leader and preacher, and the superintendent is a member of the congregation; and, finally, the superintendent is a member of the church fellowship which called the minister to be its pastor, preacher, and administrator.

Technically, the superintendent is the administrator of one phase of the church life, working with the pastor, the chief administrator. In actual practice, however, most pastors and their church school superintendents seek to work as a team because of their mutual concern for the welfare of the church and its teaching program and because they respect each other's motives and hopes for the church. Even when differences of opinion may appear on specific issues, if there is a basic respect for each other, such differences can be resolved. Patience, prayer, and mutual regard can do much where pastor and superintendent recognize and appreciate the devotion and integrity of each other.

The pastor and superintendent will not decide policy

changes in the functioning of the school. Those are matters for the board of Christian education to work out. As ex-officio members of the board, however, both pastor and superintendent have the opportunity to suggest in board meetings such policy changes as they may consider advisable. They likewise share in the decisions of the board.

There are many practical details in the work of the school in which the superintendent and the pastor can be of help to each other. The superintendent will find it helpful to draw on the pastor's experience in previous situations or may find in their mutual explorations of various possibilities that answers can be worked out together that neither could have reached separately.

The church and its Sunday school have a responsibility for ministering to the same persons. The superintendent and the pastor, working together, can do much to give the teaching program a significant place in the total life of the church. This will assist the board to enlist top-quality personnel for its leadership and to provide adequate teaching materials, equipment, and space. With pastor and superintendent working as a team, both are enriched through the relationship. Technically, of course, decisions officially guiding the superintendent in the work are made by the board of Christian education, not by the superintendent and pastor working apart from the board. The finest values in the superintendent-pastor relationship lie not so much in official directives as in the mutual sharing of a common responsibility for the spiritual nurture of children, youth, and adults.

5. *The Director of Christian Education:* If a church has a director of Christian education, the relationship between the superintendent and the director is similar

to that existing between the superintendent and the pastor. It is expected, of course, that the director will be a person thoroughly trained in the field of Christian education, and one competent, therefore, not only to direct the total educational program of the church but also to give expert guidance to those who work with him or her, such as the superintendent of the Sunday school and the counselors of the youth groups.

The basic policies of the church in regard to its educational program are determined by the board of Christian education. What then, are the relationships of the board, the director of Christian education, and the superintendent of the Sunday school to the various phases of the church's educational program? Let us use the area of leadership education as an illustration. The board member responsible for an effective church program of leader development will find the director of real value in terms of guidance and administration. In setting up or directing such a program, the superintendent will point out the leadership needs of the school and tell what she or he hopes may be accomplished by the program.

Again, the director of Christian education will guide and assist the personnel committee of the board in discovering and enlisting persons for the various tasks connected with the educational program of the church. The superintendent will make known to the board the leadership personnel needs of the Sunday school. As a member of the board, the superintendent will have a voice in the selection and approval of the persons chosen as workers.

This, in general, defines the respective fields of service filled by the superintendent and the director of Christian education. In a specific situation, these relationships will be worked out to the best advantage of the teaching program of the church.

6. *The Board of Christian Education:* The board of Christian education is the board to which the superintendent is directly responsible. Whether elected by the church or appointed by the board, the superintendent reports regularly to the board and brings to its attention the needs as well as the achievements of the school.

The superintendent will find that the board gives much of its time, thought, and effort to the Sunday school. Because of the administrative relationship to the school, the superintendent's analysis of its needs and suggestions for meeting them will carry considerable weight with the board. Close cooperation with the board can develop into an effective leadership pattern.

The superintendent, by virtue of an intimate knowledge of the Sunday school, will be able to make a significant contribution to the work of the board, particularly as it relates to the Sunday school. At the same time, through the connection with the board, the superintendent will gain a greater appreciation of the total education program of the church and of the relationship between the Sunday school and the other phases of the church's educational work. The youth fellowship evening program, for example, and its relationship to the Sunday school will be better understood by the superintendent functioning as a member of the board of Christian education. The age-group committees of the board of Christian education will work closely with the superintendent of the school as they give consideration to the special needs of the specific age divisions for which they are responsible. Such age-group committees do not function in executive or administrative capacity within the Sunday school. Their findings and suggestions are brought to the board for consideration as it fashions the policies and makes the decisions that guide the superintendent in administrative responsibility. Such committees can be a source of much practical help.

The church librarian usually serves under the jurisdiction of the board of Christian education, possibly as a member of the Committee on Leader Development. Again, however, the superintendent will find that the library and its librarian can be helpful in furnishing workers on a loan basis with books and magazines that will stimulate their development and increase their ability. The superintendent will be wise to emphasize the values of the library both in contacts with workers and in the board meetings where budgetary matters are determined. A good library, constantly used, can be a big asset to the Sunday school.

7. *Church and Community Relationships:* As the official head of the Sunday school, the superintendent will have occasion from time to time to represent the school in its participation in other church activities, as well as in interchurch activities in the community. At times such extra responsibilities may seem burdensome, but by participating, one can make an important contribution to the morale of the school. If there is any question in one's own mind as to the wisdom of participation in a specific event or project as official representative of the Sunday school, it will be helpful to turn to the board of Christian education for counsel.

8. *The Superintendent's Staff:* The number of those who make up the staff of the Sunday school will vary with the size of the school. A school with an attendance under seventy-five will probably have a staff of several teachers, a secretary, and possibly a treasurer and an

assistant superintendent. A larger school may well add not only additional teachers but also departmental or divisional superintendents, secretaries, and possibly other assistant superintendents.

The larger the school, the more indirect becomes the relationship between the general superintendent and the teachers. Yet, as indicated earlier, that relationship is important; and the superintendent will maintain the morale of the teachers through relationships with them, through public references to them, and through appreciation expressed for their work from time to time.

In a larger school, the superintendent will work closely with the departmental or divisional superintendents. Schools with two or more classes within a departmental classification (Nursery, Kindergarten, Primary, etc.) are usually organized into departmental units of several classes, with a departmental superintendent in charge of each unit. In some schools, the organization may be on the basis of a children's division, a youth division, and an adult division.

Such departmental or divisional superintendents give constant supervision to the work of their teachers and classes, possibly leading or planning worship, noting curriculum materials and resources needed, and keeping the general superintendent informed as to the basic program and the possibilities for improving it. Such persons are part of the superintendent's executive staff. Because of their close relationship to the teachers and students, their observations and suggestions are significant. The alert superintendent will profit by them. Although technically the departmental superintendents are subordinate to the general superintendent, they will build a finer school, with a more wholesome morale, if treated as partners rather than as subordinates. A superintendent can learn much from departmental leaders.

The secretary, or secretaries, in most schools have three major responsibilities: (a) correspondence, (b) record keeping, and (c) ordering and distributing supplies. In a small school these responsibilities may be handled by one person. In a very large school, a general secretary with three assistants may discharge these duties. In the average school, one secretary handles correspondence and orders supplies, and the other keeps the records of the school.

The Sunday church school superintendent will find the work of the secretary, or secretaries, of much help in the smooth and efficient functioning of the school. Records are important, although the answer to the question of *how important* depends in large measure on the relevance of the records to the work of the school. It is sound policy to examine and evaluate periodically the method of record keeping and the type of information recorded. Some record keeping may be a compiling of facts used by no one. On the other hand, information may be needed that is not now being recorded.

The ordering and distributing of supplies have an important bearing on the morale of the school. Inadequate or insufficient materials create within the teaching staff a feeling of nonsupport. Supplies that arrive late, due to delay in ordering, produce irritation, or ultimately, indifference.

The above reasons make clear the importance of the work done by the secretaries. The superintendent, therefore, will recognize those secretaries whose work is noteworthy and give guidance to those who need suggestions for improvement.

The treasurer needs to be accurate as well as honest.

Promptness in the payment of bills, care in charging expenses to appropriate budgetary items, accuracy in keeping financial records—all these make a good treasurer a joy to have in the administration of the school. The requirements are few, but absolutely necessary. A wise superintendent will give thanks for a good treasurer and a valuable co-worker.

Even in a small school, the superintendent will do well to have an assistant, if for no other reason than to train someone for future responsibility. In a small school, the superintendent will probably have the assistant share in a variety of responsibilities to provide thorough training in many different phases of the work.

In a larger school, assistants are sometimes assigned specialized responsibilities under the supervision of the general superintendent. One assistant, for example, could be in charge of personnel: (1) be responsible for seeing that each department and class has a full staff of workers present each Sunday; (2) keep the superintendent informed of personnel needs.

Another assistant might be concerned with membership: (1) use attendance records to follow up on absentees and help maintain regular attendance of enrolled students; (2) discover ways of recruiting new students, finding help in recruitment programs published by the denomination.

Yet another assistant might be in charge of special resources and equipment: (1) report and/or procure needed supplies or equipment requested by teachers or departmental superintendents; (2) study and recommend new resources such as audiovisual aids, analyzing their worth and suitability for use in the Sunday school in the light of teaching goals and procedures.

Such assistants would work in close cooperation

with the general superintendent, reporting their findings and suggestions to be relayed to the board of Christian education for due consideration.

In this chapter we have sought to indicate the significant personal relationships of the general superintendent in the leadership of the Sunday school. Obviously, in all such relationships, the general suggestions that have been made will be complicated or strengthened by the personality, qualities, and attitudes of each person involved. Under all circumstances, however, the superintendent will find it helpful to read and digest 1 Corinthians 13:4-7. One of the modern translations may be helpful.

Chapter 5

Leader Development in the Sunday School

Leader development is an important facet of the program of Christian education in most local churches. The board or committee of Christian education, through its coordinator of leader development, will be responsible for planning the ongoing program of training for all educational leaders. This includes arranging for leadership classes or workshops within the congregation and promoting attendance at events in the community or sponsored by the denomination. The superintendent of the Sunday school works with the coordinator of leader development to plan, implement, and promote a leadership training program for Sunday school teachers and staff.

Whether they are called teacher meetings, staff councils, workers' conferences, or some other title, these gatherings provide the occasion when the Sunday school teachers and leaders confer concerning their work: its purpose, its achievements, its failures, and the use of more effective ways of achieving its goals and objectives.

The Sunday school superintendent knows that every moment spent in planning a worthwhile meeting and in enlisting the 100 percent attendance of Sunday school workers is time well spent. It contributes to a stronger school by achieving several objectives:

Value of the Teachers' Meeting

1. *Recognition:* A Sunday school worker, when properly recruited, is impressed with the fact of making a contribution to a significant expression of the church's life—its Christian teaching program. The teachers' meeting emphasizes the importance of the teaching program and each leader's

A Teachers' Meeting Provides
Recognition
Fellowship
Improvement
Inspiration
Planning

contribution to it. Furthermore, as the various phases of the school's program come under consideration, achievements are noted; recognition of individual as well as group achievement constitutes one value of such a gathering.

2. *Fellowship:* True fellowship grows out of a genuine concern for a shared interest or mutual responsibility. The Sunday school teacher shares with co-workers a concern for the success of one's own efforts and, consciously or unconsciously, for the success of the school as a whole. Therefore, each person needs fellowship with co-workers from time to time, especially since much of the work of teaching is done separately from them.

Whereas the teacher of a class, for example, participates in the fellowship of that class, and perhaps with a team teacher, each works alone so far as co-workers in the school are concerned. Casual meetings with other teachers and the momentary exploration of their experiences serve only to accentuate the basic lack of more frequent fellowship in their common responsibilities. The regular schedule of teachers' meetings insures frequent occasions for the fellowship so vital to the continuing morale of the school's workers.

3. *Improvement:* Teachers' meetings can be of help in stimulating the desire for improvement and in showing the way by which it can be achieved. Where the school is large enough, departmental conferences will be concerned with practical ways in which improvement can be made within the departments. But individual improvement, as well as that of the school as a whole, should be a major concern of the general meeting. The year's program can be planned to provide specific elements leading to the improvement of the school and of the individual teachers and officers. A portion of the program may be a leadership training course, or there may be a series of sessions concerned with those phases of the school's program which stand in the greatest need of improvement.

4. *Inspiration:* A successful teachers' meeting will send out its workers inspired to do better work—not merely with a recognition that better work is needed or with only an understanding of how it might be done. There needs to be a strong conviction that the work can and must be done, and that there is a joy to be found in the doing of it. Occasionally an outside speaker may bring an inspirational message; more frequently, however, the stimulus will come from the nature and atmosphere of the meeting itself. If the program elements seem truly relevant to the teachers, and if they open vistas of new and better approaches to their tasks, the conference will serve to bring enduring inspiration to the workers.

The worship phase of the program can bring spiritual uplift, with emphasis on the fact that we are not only workers, and workers together, but also workers together with God.

5. *Planning:* Most administrative details lie in the hands of the board of Christian education or officers of the Sunday school. However, there are administrative concerns, policies, and decisions that directly affect the teachers. Such matters merit discussion, understanding, and evaluation by the Sunday school workers, particularly where the success of such policies and decisions depends in large measure upon their full cooperation.

Although decisions about curriculum, grading, space, and time schedules are made by the board of Christian education, all these matters need to be adequately interpreted to the teachers and discussed by them. Such matters should be carefully outlined and factually supported before being brought up for consideration. If teachers are expected to understand the objectives of the school and work together to achieve them, they need opportunities to share in the planning. Out of such discussion and planning will come an awareness of the problem areas that need more thorough consideration; these may become subjects for further systematic study by the group.

Organization

An effective teachers' meeting depends on adequate planning and preparation. The superintendent of the Sunday school, as the administrative leader of the school, is responsible for the success of these meetings. This does not mean that one person alone prepares and conducts the programs, but that he or she, as leader of the school, cannot afford to have weak or ineffective meetings.

1. *Leadership:* The superintendent, or someone designated, will preside at the teachers' meetings. A program committee, consisting of the general superintendent, the coordinator of leader development for the church, and possibly representatives from the children's, youth, and adult divisions of the Sunday school will plan the meeting.

2. *Attendance:* Strive for 100 percent attendance of all persons serving in the school. This includes teachers and substitutes, department or divisional superintendents or coordinators, the general superintendent, the director of Christian education, and the pastor. Additional staff members such as assistant superintendents, secretaries, treasurer, and librarian are also encouraged to participate.

Realistically, it might be well to identify at the beginning of the Sunday school year the number of local teachers' meetings that will be held. State the expectation of your church that teachers attend at least a designated percentage of these meetings. This approach recognizes the busy lifestyles of adults while communicating reasonable expectations.

3. *Frequency:* Experimentation and experience will usually determine the frequency most helpful for the persons involved in each local congregation. In one church, regular evening meetings, such as the second Tuesday, will be most convenient. In another church, a monthly Sunday breakfast meeting with child care provided meets the teachers' needs. Teachers in a third church choose to meet following Sunday worship for a designated period of time. Yet a fourth group meets weekly for Bible study to prepare for the following Sunday. It is good to establish a regular and definite

time so that participants can reserve the date and time and keep it free of conflicts.

Although frequent and regular meetings are beneficial, a superintendent will work with what is feasible. A quarterly evening meeting of longer duration may be possible for some. Others may find brief but more frequent sessions will meet some of the needs for training and sharing information. A combination of these may prove best of all.

Although some churches discontinue the meetings in the summer, other churches have capitalized on this period for review of the previous year's work and for planning the work for the year to come.

4. *Time Schedule:* The time schedule for the teachers' meeting can be arranged in any one of several ways. If, for example, a leadership training course is to be the program feature for a series of six workers' conferences, fifty minutes may be allowed for it. For other program features, thirty to forty minutes may be sufficient. On some occasions a major change in school policy will make it wise to combine the time usually devoted to a program feature with that reserved for the discussion of policies and needs, thereby making available a full hour or more of time.

5. *Location:* Occasionally it may seem wise, because of local conditions or the size of the group, to hold the meeting in a home. Such a setting usually adds much to the feeling of fellowship. Unless care is exercised, however, the fellowship may profit at the expense of constructive work.

Most teachers' meetings are held in the church. It is important to choose a room that is adequate but not too large. A group lost in a large room is apt to feel equally lost in its search for fellowship with one another. On the other hand, a group cramped in a little room may react with unconscious or conscious irritation that will color the proceedings adversely. The superintendent will do well to see that the room is adequate in size, properly ventilated, neat, clean, and well lighted. These seemingly trivial matters will do much toward the success of the meeting.

Planning the Program

The program factors in a teachers' meeting are worship, the program feature, discussion of current school policies and needs, and departmental conferences, as

Program Factors Are
Worship
Program Feature
Discussion: Policies and Needs
Departmental Planning

needed. Variety in content of these factors will usually grow out of the changing conditions of the school and the seasons of the year.

1. *Worship:* The theme for worship will be related to and develop from the program feature, either preceding or following it. Worship leadership with a creative concern for its worth can bring a spiritual dimension to the whole teachers' meeting. The next chapter contains guidance for planning worship. In addition, excellent suggestions can be found in denominational magazines and other worship resource materials.

2. *Program Feature:* This may be a leadership training session, a thorough consideration of a major policy change, a session for review and planning, a Bible study related to teaching topics, or a guest speaker. This, as well as the other program factors, grows out of the needs and interests, opportunities, and problems of the teachers. The themes for this feature are almost unlimited.

The teachers may be asked to indicate the areas in which they feel the greatest need of help. A sample assessment form is provided in Appendix 5; adapt and revise it to fit your local situation.

Explore the field of leader development courses sponsored by the Christian education department of your denomination. Choose one or a series that is most appropriate for your teachers.

Organize a series of programs around the goal for the Sunday school, a response to the use of the evaluation form "Characteristics of Effective and Vital Christian Education," or the Standard of Achievement.

When a school's curriculum materials focus on a unified theme for all ages in the church school, Bible studies related to these topics can be particularly helpful and relevant. The pastor who leads these studies helps strengthen the foundations of the church's teaching ministry. Whether presented as a monthly or quarterly topic, such a biblical emphasis provides useful background for the teaching staff.

Whatever the annual theme for the program feature, it is advisable to devote a session to review and planning: review the achievements and failures of the past year and plan the principal objectives for the year to come. Devote time to considering special ways by which the coming year's objectives will be attained. A special meal, picnic, or other celebrative event may conclude the sequence of teacher meetings.

Many resources are available to help those responsible for this phase of the teachers' meeting. For example, one denomination prepares each year a series of twelve workers' conference programs. Detailed suggestions and resources for each program appear in the denominational teachers' magazine for the month prior to the conference in which the theme will be used. Another denomination places an emphasis on the concept of the "teaching church." It has focused on the five functions of the teaching church:

> to affirm the foundations of its teaching ministry;
> to plan for the most effective teaching ministry;
> to develop leaders for a variety of ministries;
> to nurture persons in Christian growth;
> to support the fulfillment of the church's mission in the world.

Program subjects, responsive to the practical and developmental needs of teachers, might include topics such as these:

> Methods—A Means to Creative Teaching
> The Technique of Team Teaching
> Planning for the Class Session
> Using Role Playing Effectively in Your Class
> The Teacher and Evangelism

A descriptive list of prepared workshops that can be led by the pastor or other experienced teacher or leader may be obtained from regional or national denominational leaders in Christian education.[9]

3. *Discussion: Policies and Needs:* Policies, problems, needs, and opportunities peculiar to the school itself constitute the third factor. Provide time for considering the decisions of the board of Christian education as they affect the work of the Sunday school. Matters on which the judgment of the workers is needed before decisions are reached will be brought up at this point.

Teachers will also have an opportunity to offer suggestions for the improvement of the school. When crucial decisions are being made, it is important to have the supporting and opposing facts ready for presentation. After decisions have been made, it is vital that the appropriate person or group responsible for carrying out the decision be made aware of the assignment.

The discussion of current school policies and needs grows out of (1) recommendations or requests from the board of Christian education, (2) special days and occasions in the church school, (3) suggestions from the school staff. Plan a detailed agenda prior to the meeting and have the information available for intelligent and profitable discussion. Inform workers in advance about matters to be considered.

4. *Departmental Conferences*: A planning period may be the fourth factor in the meeting's content. Planning time for matters pertaining specifically to departments, or children, youth, and adult divisions, could be provided quarterly or as needed, to help meet situations unique to each age group. When conclusions that concern the entire school are reached, share them with the appropriate personnel for further consideration and action. Department superintendents or age level coordinators who are in charge of this part of the program will need to plan carefully in order to use the time profitably.

Teachers' meetings are the power-center for an effective Sunday school staff. Encourage every worker to attend; then guide them by means of an engaging and helpful program that will make them glad they came.

In addition to teachers' meetings, workshops, and classes, superintendents can use other ways to equip persons to do their tasks more effectively. These include recommending specific articles in periodicals or helpful portions of books to read, encouraging visits with experienced friends, and briefing sessions you hold with a person to help them prepare for doing a specific task.

Retreats, week-long summer conferences, videocassettes, observation of others, case studies, in-service training, mentoring, supervision, and evaluation are some additional ways of providing support and encouragement for teachers to continue to grow in specific skills and abilities.

Chapter 6

The Spiritual Life of the Sunday School

If the superintendent is to guide the school in its emphasis on the reality of the presence and power of God in life, that experience must be real in the person's own life. A superintendent may make errors in administrative judgment and yet, because of genuine dedication and devotion to the work, be the leader of a growing and effective school. On the other hand, excellence of organizational structure cannot make amends for spiritual insincerity or apathy.

The Superintendent and the Spiritual Life of the School

One basic way by which the superintendent may influence the spiritual life of the Sunday school is through the reality of one's own growing spiritual life.

The personal disciplines of Bible study, prayer, and meditation reflect a reliance upon God and a trust in the wisdom of the Almighty. Based on the value of one's own personal experiences, the superintendent will seek to encourage personal spiritual growth and worship for all teachers and staff. Providing or suggesting resources, such as *The Secret Place* or some other daily devotional material, will be helpful. Some curriculum materials suggest daily Bible readings related to the study theme. Topics related to worship, such as developing a deeper prayer life, may be the basis for an occasional class or workshop for Sunday school workers.

As part of a yearly theme established at the fall meeting of teachers and staff, specific Scriptures, monthly or seasonal topics, or the use of a common devotional resource may be planned. A variety of prayer disciplines or keeping a spiritual journal are other forms that might be suggested.

In the second place, the superintendent will keep constantly before the teachers, as well as before the entire church constituency, the school's emphasis upon Christian commitment and growth in Christian character and influence. This may be done not only in the teachers' meetings but also from time to time on informal occasions and in public meetings. If the denomination has one over-all objective in Christian education, it may be adopted as the stated objective of the Sunday school and be made familiar to the whole church, as well as to the Sunday school leaders. In addition to publishing it in the church bulletin for Christian Education Week, make frequent reference to it throughout the year. It will serve as a standard by which suggestions for changes in the Sunday school curriculum or practices are judged. In addition, it will help to make clear that the basic objective of the Sunday school is really the basic objective of the total church fellowship.

In the third place, the superintendent who would emphasize the essential spiritual purpose of the Sunday school can accomplish much by encouraging the departmental superintendents and other workers responsible for worship to recognize the value and significance of worship for the whole program of Christian education. True worship grows out of reactions to experiences. Worship which is related to, or grows out of, other Christian educational experiences is capable of being made the best kind of worship. The departmental superintendent or other worship leader will be alert to these opportunities.

Particularly with younger children, it is helpful to encourage teachers to respond to spontaneous expressions of worship during the class session, taking advantage of these teachable moments.

Whenever the superintendent is in charge of a worship service, the spiritual realities in the life of the members of the school can be strengthened by a careful personal preparation of that service and by a reverent attitude when leading it. In these ways one reveals an appreciation of its importance. The casual or hasty last-minute search for hymns or the stumbling reading of an ill-digested Scripture passage not only drains the life out of the worship service but also proclaims in unmistakable terms that worship is merely a trivial tradition of empty value. On the other hand, a thoughtfully prepared service, led in reverent spirit, can make worship a memorable moment in the spiritual growth of everyone participating.

The superintendent will find it a profitable experience, personally and also for the school, to make a study of worship: its nature, its rich resources, and its many possible variations. The results of this study will be helpful on those occasions when one is personally responsible for leading worship; they will also be of service when one is called on to train others in the preparation and leadership of worship services.

Finally, the superintendent can influence the spiritual life of the Sunday school through building up that section of the church library that deals with worship, including its department of audiovisual aids. New teachers will be introduced to the library and encouraged to make use of it. The superintendent may find it helpful to enlist some person to become a resource person in worship, ready to assist other Sunday school leaders in discovering more effective ways of guiding the worship of their groups.

Worship in the Sunday School

The superintendent, along with members of the board or committee of Christian education and with input from teachers and other staff, has the responsibility for determining how worship will be related to the Sunday school program. A variety of options are possible.

Some churches make use of a unified service of worship and study and emphasize the value of families attending the church worship service together as the foundation experience for the graded educational program of the church. Such a program does not require a general assembly of the school, as the church worship service is the school at worship, even as the class sessions are the church at study.

In churches with a different format for worship and study, all of the church school classes, separate departments, or individual classes may gather for worship at either the beginning or close of the Sunday school session.

In combination with any of these, teachers may be encouraged and trained to recognize and take advantage of spontaneous moments of worship in the midst of a class session.

Whatever the groupings, it is important to be clear about the reasons for worship gatherings. Some may emphasize the importance of a total and intergenerational Sunday school gathering. As a preparation for study, worship can help students by encouraging them to be conscious of God's presence. As a conclusion to study time, worship offers opportunity for confession and perhaps dedication of oneself or commitment to a specific course of action.

Worship in the Sunday school will be most beneficial for those involved when the time and form are consciously determined, not done out of habit or because that is the way it always has been done. Gatherings larger than a single class may be held weekly, monthly, quarterly, or seasonally (Rally Day, Christmas, Easter, and so forth). Although the integration of worship and study is difficult when there is not uniformity among individual class study topics, seasonal themes may be chosen and the worship assemblies held less frequently.

When planning worship for a broad age range, it is vital to recognize the presence of children. If the service is planned so that its various parts are meaningful to them, everyone will benefit by the service; whereas, if the service is planned for adults only, it will have little constructive value for children and youth. The Bible passages, hymns, prayers, and interpretation are all selected not only because of their appropriateness to the worship theme but also because of their worth for all ages.

The superintendent might assign to individuals of the various age-groups parts of the worship service so that many may receive experience in conducting worship. Also, occasionally a class might be asked to plan and conduct the worship service.

Pictures may often be used effectively as the focal point of a worship center. If from time to time the picture expressing the worship theme is chosen from the picture sets used in the children's classes, this will indicate that the younger participants in the service are being considered.

Music, pictures, and stories will enrich and add variety to the worship. The superintendent, when planning a worship service, will find useful the general suggestions given later in this chapter in the section entitled "Elements of Worship." In the assembly period eliminate or keep to a minimum matters of business and announcements. This will improve the worship experience and also allow more time for the class session.

In churches where Sunday school worship is usually on a divisional, departmental, or class basis, the superintendent does not customarily have direct responsibility for Sunday school worship but will want to be familiar with the practices within the school's graded worship program and do everything possible to encourage the recognition of their value and importance.

Worship in the Meetings of Sunday School Staff

In Chapter 5 it was recommended that worship be included in every teachers' meeting or training program. The superintendent, as chairperson of these teachers' meetings, is directly responsible for seeing that worship is planned and conducted as a regular part of the program. The superintendent can enhance the value of the worship in all of the Sunday school departments through the emphasis placed on worship in the teachers' meetings. The worship service need not be long; usually ten to fifteen minutes is sufficient. It should, however, be prepared thoughtfully and with imaginative use of varied resources.

The worship at meetings of Sunday school staff, therefore, becomes the superintendent's opportunity not only to provide genuine worship experience but also to demonstrate what worship is at its best. For these reasons, the worship services of the workers' conferences will be carefully planned and in keeping with the theme. The superintendent will work closely with the program committee in preparation of the program, including the worship.

The superintendent of the Sunday school, whether the school be small or large, will find it wise to keep in mind that there are certain basic elements that contribute to effective worship. By becoming increasingly familiar with these elements and discovering their unlimited possibilities, the superintendent will also realize how central worship is in the Christian education ministry of the school and be better able also to counsel department superintendents and others respecting the improvement of worship.

The Elements of Worship

1. *Attitudes:* Attitudes open the doors by which God enters our lives. Worship makes for better attitudes. The attitude of the worship leader will do much to determine the attitude of the

Worship Elements Include
Attitudes
Setting
Program Factors
Resource Materials
Creative Imagination

other worshipers. We say, "We should be reverent," but what does true reverence involve?

Expectancy is a part of reverence. The conviction that the worship experience is real, that something significant is happening, and that we are privileged to share in it—all this is a part of true worship.

Receptiveness also is a part of true worship. The recognition that God is reaching out to us, even as we are reaching out to God, is basic. When this attitude is real, then worship is real.

Sincerity is fundamental to worship. There are few things, if any, that so quickly block the channel of fellowship with God as does insincerity. Sincerity of spirit makes it possible for worship to be genuine; and it must be genuine if it is to be helpful.

Commitment is implicit in worship. We worship God because basically we recognize as valid in all the other relationships of life the implications of our personal and group commitment. Worship is a constant renewal of that commitment to God.

Fulfillment is the outcome of worship. Whether we desire to share gratitude, to ask forgiveness, to gain strength, or to seek wisdom, worship finds its indication of effectiveness in fulfillment.

These, then, are the attitudes that create reverence, the mood for worship. The worship leader who exhibits these attitudes has a better opportunity of communicating them to others.

2. *Setting:* Because we are not disembodied spirits, we are influenced by the setting in which our experiences take place. This is true of worship; the setting is important.

The room, with its color, its lighting, its ventilation, its furniture, and its seating arrangement, is either depressing or conducive to worship. A room in order, neatly and attractively furnished, well lighted but not glaring, well ventilated but not drafty, is obviously an aid to those worshiping.

The worship center itself must be easily seen by all present. Whatever objects or symbols are used in it will be suitable to the worship theme and expressive of it. Religious pictures, the Bible, flowers, the cross, and candles are among the traditional symbols used.

See that accessories, such as hymnals, musical instruments, reading stand or pulpit, and Bibles, are kept in first-class condition. Hymnals with loose pages or broken covers, pianos with off-key notes, and littered tables obviously add in no way to the experience of worship, particularly for those new members or visitors not blinded or deafened by familiarity with them.

3. *Program Factors:* If worship is central to the spiritual vitality of the church's educational program, prayer is central to worship. Prayer may take many forms: silent prayer, brief prayers from several participants, spoken prayer by the leader or some designated person, and guided prayer. Prayer is evidence that we believe in the reality of our conscious relationship with God and are ready to share in it.

Hymns constitute another factor in programming for worship. With the large number of hymns available—hymns that cover a vast range of Christian experience—there is no reason to use any but the best. Select hymns that are appropriate for the age of the participants, both theologically and musically. The hymnal, next to the Bible, will prove to be the superintendent's most versatile program resource. Hymns may be used in singing, in prayer, in commenting on Bible verses, and in the interpretation of Christian life and character. They may be sung, they may be read, they may be hummed, or they may be played instrumentally.

The Bible, of course, is the basic source book of our faith, and from its pages come passages of true inspiration and worship. Some passages are more suitable for worship than are others; some selections are more expressive of group aspirations than others; and obviously some sections relate to the worship theme more closely than do others. As familiarity with the Bible increases, a superintendent will discover more sections that can be appropriately used in worship.

The interpretation of the worship theme may take any one of many forms. It may be a story, a poem, or a reading which is related to the Scripture passage; it may be a hymn, a solo, a duet, or an anthem; it may center in the worship symbol or picture; or it may be a brief message.

When an offering is included, it should definitely be considered an act of worship—an expression of dedication, commitment, and participation in some phase of God's purpose.

The following may be a guide when considering the progression of worship elements within a service: adoration, confession, thanksgiving, supplication, and dedication. For children, these elements are expressed in the following phrases: I love you, God; I am sorry; thank you for . . . ; please help . . . ; and God, I will. . . . Any one or more of the program factors may be used to present the various worship elements.

4. *Resource Materials:* In addition to the Bible and the hymnal, several other sources of worship materials are available. Some denominational magazines provide suggestions for teachers' worship services, as well as for graded worship in the Sunday school. It is important to use materials that appropriately reflect the familiar experiences of the participants, particularly children.

Devotional booklets, such as *The Secret Place* and *The Upper Room*, frequently contain stories adaptable for worship services. The many devotional books which are constantly coming off the presses may be similarly used. In addition, there is a rapidly growing number of books specifically prepared as resource books for worship services.

Another growing field of worship resources is that of audiovisual aids. If these are used as aids to worship, they can be most helpful.

Even as the church library should include books and magazines to aid worship leaders in their planning, so the church school will find it helpful to build up a collection of mounted pictures, slides, audiocassette tapes, compact disks, videocassette tapes, and so forth, that will be available when needed.

A different classification of resource materials lies within the Christian or church year itself. Christmas, Easter, Pentecost, Mother's Day, Children's Day, Father's Day, and our national holidays all have a rich heritage of stories that can contribute to the worship experience.

A final resource for effective worship lies within the various persons in your church who can share in the leadership of worship. When another person (child, youth, or adult) is asked to take part by reading the Scripture passage or by leading in prayer, the time taken to coach this participant to do one's best will add much to the effectiveness of the service. Well-prepared persons are among the greatest worship resources a superintendent can use!

5. *Creative Imagination in Worship:* Almost every printed worship program will need adaptation if it is to be of greatest value. Differences in physical equipment, setting, worship resources, individuals and groups, and the worship leaders themselves all condition what aids worship most in a specific situation. A

recognition of this fundamental fact, together with a willingness to harness the imagination creatively, can work wonders with even the most commonplace worship suggestions.

First, examine a suggested worship service and analyze it in the light of suggestions made earlier in this chapter. For a beginner in the art of worship preparation, this is usually, at first, a sounder approach than making a completely new program.

Second, in the light of the suggested worship theme, make the necessary changes in the program to fit your particular needs. You know your local situation and the group you are leading. Are there good hymns in your hymnal that are more apt than those suggested? As for the Scripture reading, do you know a more appropriate selection, or is there a more impressive way of including it in the service? Can it best be included as a solo reading, as a unison reading, or as a responsive reading? How helpful would it be to present it in the form of a litany or through a speech-choir rendering?

How can the prayer experience be made most vital to those participating in the service? Which will be the best procedure: a guided prayer, brief sentence prayers, silent prayer, prayer by the leader, or a combination of these?

Finally, how can the transition from the group experience to worship be made most effectively and smoothly? From worship to the next group experience? Does music help?

The search for answers to the above questions should stimulate the alert superintendent to use creative imagination in improving the worship of the Sunday school, thereby strengthening its spiritual life.

Appendix 1

Questions and Projects

The following questions and projects may be used in several ways:

1. for independent study, to help direct your thinking, or to focus attention on particular areas of need;

2. for group discussion in a local church, perhaps by members of the board of Christian education or Sunday school staff or a designated task force working on a specific topic;

3. in a leader development course, to focus group discussion or as assignments between sessions.

Chapter 1

1. List the qualifications of a good superintendent.

2. Recall two or three situations in which you believe you were helpful to workers whom you counseled.

3. Describe your plan for improving your spiritual life.

4. Make a list of your responsibilities as superintendent of your Sunday school. Check those which you have been carrying out. Think of ways by which you can include other duties in order to increase your effectiveness as a superintendent.

5. Note the six "elements" mentioned in this chapter as part of the superintendent's work. Select the factor in which you are weakest or the one which is most needed in your school, and make a study of it. Determine specific action steps you will take.

Chapter 2

1. Be prepared to make a three-minute talk or write a page on the importance of the teaching of the Bible as a means of spreading the gospel.

2. Work with the board of Christian education to analyze your church's goal statement for educational ministry. Develop two specific objectives for improving your program, including the steps to be taken, the time frame for accomplishing these steps, and who is responsible for each action. List the resources needed, ways to inform the church membership, and what means will be used to check on the accomplishment of the objectives.

3. Make a survey of the curriculum materials being used in your Sunday school and list your findings for each age level or department. Evaluate these findings in the light of the criteria set up by the author. Indicate improvements which you would recommend.

4. Evaluate your present equipment and, on the basis of equipment needs, make recommendations for purchases.

Chapter 3

1. Assuming that the board of Christian education has responsibility for enlisting and training workers, discuss the personnel who would select the following: (a) a primary teacher for a Sunday school, (b) the superintendent of the Junior High Department, (c) the general superintendent, (d) the pianist in the adult department.

2. List the most helpful ways to train your teachers.

3. Be prepared to explain how your Sunday school is organized.

4. Discuss the use made of the records kept by your Sunday school.

5. Prepare a time schedule for a Sunday school with several departments or for a one-room school. Indicate the time you think would be given to each of the following: (a) worship, (b) the class session, (c) record keeping, (d) fellowship, (e) other items.

6. During the next two Sundays carry out the following survey in all departments (or, at least, in one department or class of the children's division, youth division, and adult division) of your Sunday school: (a) record the time each group began, (b) note how many teachers and officers were on time or present in advance of the time scheduled for opening and those who were late or absent without adequate preparation being made by other persons to take over their work.

Chapter 4

1. Discuss the statement "The superintendent is a symbol of the Sunday school."

2. What is the relationship of the superintendent to the pastor? to the church director of Christian education? to the general secretary, the assistant superintendent, and the other officers?

3. Write a paragraph on how a good superintendent cooperates with the board of Christian education. Suggest ways by which the board can make the work of the superintendent easier.

Chapter 5

1. List several values of holding teachers' meetings.

2. Who plans the programs?

3. About how much time is spent on the various phases of the teachers' meetings held in your church,

such as the worship, business, and main feature? What changes in the time schedule do you believe would benefit your programs? Prepare a detailed program for one teachers' meeting, including the time schedule.

4. Suggest a theme for a year's teachers' meeting programs for your Sunday school and list possible monthly titles.

Chapter 6

1. What is the responsibility of the superintendent in connection with the worship experience of a Sunday school which is fully departmentalized? in a school with departments organized in the children's division only? in a one-room school?

2. Discuss worship as related to meetings of Sunday school staff.

3. What elements are included in a good worship service?

4. Plan a service of worship for use with a group with which you arc connected.

Characteristics of Effective and Vital Christian Education[10]

Evaluation Form

Planning for Effective and Vital Christian Education

1. Rate your congregation's Christian education by putting the appropriate numeral on the blank to the left of each statement:

> 1 = strong
> 2 = adequate
> 3 = needs improvement

Note that there is space to add additional descriptive statements for each characteristic.

2. Review your ratings and star (*) the one or two (not more than 3!) needing attention first.

3. Jot down concerns you have or steps you think could be taken.

Characteristics of Effective and Vital Christian Education

1. The church gives priority to Christian education (CE) and understands that it is more than just Sunday school.

___ adequate financial support given

___ frequent mention of CE in public places (bulletin, bulletin board, newsletter, etc.)

___ adequate time set aside for formal CE

___ informal teaching and learning recognized and affirmed

___ Christian education takes place in a variety of settings (committees, choirs, worship, special events, etc.)

2. The pastor is committed to, involved in, and trained in Christian education.

___ teaches a class or group

___ attends CE board meetings

___ openly advocates for CE

___ preaches "teaching" sermons

___ supports teachers and leaders

3. Teachers and leaders are knowledgeable, committed, caring, and teachable.

___ attend training events

___ tend to their own spiritual growth

___ spend time outside class with those they teach

___ are themselves open to learning and growing

___ know the Bible and teaching methods

___ keep abreast of current information and skills related to their responsibilities, whether teacher, group leader, committee chair, church officer, and so forth.

4. The teaching ministry with adults is given a strong emphasis.

___ choices of study offered

___ in-depth Bible study available

___ small groups provided

___ in auxiliary groups, boards (deacons, trustees, etc.), committees, choirs

5. Programs for children are offered.

___ during Sunday school

___ during the week, after school, or evening

___ weekday nursery school and/or child care

___ camping opportunities for elementary age children

___ community outreach ministries

___ choirs or musical groups

6. Programs for youth are offered.

___ classes during Sunday school

___ evening fellowship group(s)

___ camp and conference opportunities

___ choirs or musical groups

___ community outreach ministries

___ college, career, and/or job counseling

7. The content offered for study addresses:

___ biblical understanding

___ global awareness

___ moral and value issues

___ social issues

8. A variety of learning activities is used for all age levels.

___ A-V equipment available

___ resource center available

___ teachers use stories, visuals, activities, etc.

___ teachers encouraged to use a variety of methods and to try new methods

___ mission tours, work groups, and service projects included as learning activities

9. Strong administrative foundations are in place.

___ teacher/leader recruitment

___ teacher/leader recognition

___ teacher/leader training

___ teacher/leader support

___ teacher/leader faith formation (spiritual growth)

___ program goals and objectives stated and known

___ evaluation done regularly

___ governing body support strong

10. Parents and guardians are supported in their "teaching" roles.

___ family worship ideas (including special seasons such as Advent, Lent) provided

___ parenting classes offered

___ Bible study groups for parents offered

___ family, life center provided

11. Members are informed, eager, and enthusiastic about the teaching ministry.

___ tell newcomers about programs

___ invite new people to attend

___ offer to help carry out the teaching ministry

Standard of Achievement for Sunday Schools

I. Attendance Increase

A. Average attendance increased at least 5 percent (the percentage changes after the first year)

B. The use of a definite plan for the enrollment and conservation of members

II. Leadership Training

A. A training program in which 25 percent of the teachers, department superintendents, and general officers participate in one or more training events

B. A minimum of six teachers' meetings attended by 60 percent of the teachers and officers

III. Church Loyalty

A. An average of at least 60 percent of those in attendance above the primary age level participating in the church's program of Sunday morning worship (the percentage may change after the first year)

B. Regular giving to local expenses and to world mission encouraged at all age levels

IV. Bible Study

A. The Bible used as the basis for study and worship in every class

B. The message of the Bible taught through the use

of denominationally recommended teaching materials in every class

V. World Mission

A mission education program including two of the following:

A. Interpretation of three areas of the denominational program in all groups above kindergarten

B. A mission education library with current books for all ages above kindergarten, and a plan in operation for their use

C. Active participation in a graded church school of missions

VI. Community Witness

A. A definite plan of outreach or visitation to enroll the unreached

B. Completion of one or more projects in Christian social relations

VII. Decisions for Christ

A genuine concern to win all persons to Jesus Christ through:

A. Training teachers to guide their students of appropriate ages toward a decision for Christ as Lord and Savior

B. Special classes in discipleship and church membership

VIII. Spiritual Enrichment

A. A program to encourage personal and family devotional practices

B. A program for the spiritual growth of teachers and officers

IX. Church-Home Cooperation

Cooperation with the home in the Christian guidance of students in two of the following:

A. One or more visits to the home of every student

B. The use of curriculum materials for the home

C. Two or more parent-teacher meetings for cooperative planning

X. Effective Organization

A. The Sunday school related to the church through a church-elected board of Christian education

B. An appropriate plan of grouping and grading

XI. Summer Activities

A program which includes two of the following:

A. Training opportunities for Sunday school workers

B. Sunday school members encouraged to take advantage of opportunities in church camping

C. Active participation in a vacation church school

XII. Better Equipment

A. Evaluation of rooms and equipment in relation to student needs and formulation of plans for improvement

B. Definite evidence of some improvement each year

Appendix 4

Sample Organizational Patterns and Time Schedules

Within any church school, the pattern of organization depends in part on the type of educational program the church desires, and in part on the number of persons involved. For example, a school with sixty students might have six classes: one for preschool children (under 6 years); one for primary children (grades 1, 2; ages 6, 7 approximately); one for middlers (grades 3, 4; ages 8, 9 approximately); one for juniors (grades 5, 6; ages 10, 11 approximately); one for youth (junior high and senior high); and one for adults. Administratively, such a school would call for six teachers, some associate teachers and helpers, a superintendent, an assistant superintendent, and possibly a secretary-treasurer, and a pianist. Such a school is just as likely to have three adult classes and one each for preschool children, elementary children, and youth. Demographics of the community and the congregation itself will be influential factors.

There are Sunday schools that will have from five to ten adult classes, with corresponding numbers in the children's and youth division. Such schools require many teachers and helpers.

Schools are graded according to the number of students. Some standards for grading follow:

a. Nursery Department, made up of children who

range in age from birth to three years inclusive. The Nursery Department may be divided, if the numbers warrant, into two groups (birth to third birthday, and a separate group for three-year-olds); into three groups (birth to eighteen months, eighteen months to third birthday, and the three-year-olds); or into four groups (birth to twelve months, one-year-olds, two-years-olds, and three-year-olds). If these divisions still leave more than twelve to fifteen children in any one nursery room, the group should be further divided.

b. Kindergarten Department, made up of children four and five years of age. When the number of kindergarten children exceeds twelve or fifteen, the department should be divided into a four-year-old group and a five-year-old group. If the resulting age groups are still above twelve to fifteen members, further division is needed.

c. Primary Department. These children are in public school grades 1, 2 (ages 6, 7 approximately). When the number of children in this group exceeds twelve to fifteen, the group should be divided into classes according to public school grade. If this division still leaves classes exceeding twelve in membership, the large classes should be further divided.

d. Middler (or Lower Junior Department), made up of children in public school grades 3, 4 (ages 8, 9 approximately). The suggestions given for the Primary Department as to divisions into classes also apply to middlers.

e. Junior Department, made up of children in public school grades 5, 6 (ages 10, 11 approximately). The suggestions given for the Primary Department as to division into classes apply also to juniors.

f. Junior High Department, grades 7, 8, 9 (ages

12, 13, 14 approximately). When the number in this department exceeds fifteen to twenty, it should be divided for classroom work. A class of five or more junior high youths makes for effective grouping. Churches, increasingly, are finding it advisable to group according to the public school grading, with boys and girls in the same classes. This may mean a middle school grouping, such as grades 5 through 8 or 6 through 8.

g. Middle High Department, grades 9, 10 (ages 14, 15 approximately) has been created in some churches. Where this exists, the standards for junior high and senior high are adapted to the new department.

h. Senior High Department, grades 10, 11, 12 (ages 15, 16, 17 approximately). When the number exceeds twenty, it usually is wise to divide for classroom work.

i. Young Adult Department, ages 18 to 35 years. In general the same principles would prevail for the Young Adult Department as for the Adult Department.

j. Adult Department, for those above 35 years of age. The number of members in an adult or young adult class will be conditioned by several factors, including teaching methods (discussion, lecture, etc.), available leadership, study materials, room size and location, and the nature of the group (men, women, or both). An ideal number in one situation may be unwise in another. To maintain person-to-person relationships and genuine fellowship within the group, adult classes should seldom exceed fifty persons in enrollment and should not exceed thirty to thirty-five in attendance. It is better to organize new groups than to increase numerically an existing group with new members who will have little opportunity to get acquainted or to exchange ideas. Whenever membership and space permit, a church should multiply the number of its adult classes. In this way, more people are apt to be reached for Christ.

k. The Home Department. This department brings the educational ministry of the church and the Sunday school to adults who, through physical disability or necessary Sunday employment, are unable to participate regularly in the church worship and study sessions.

The school which is graded on the foregoing plan will require at least one teacher for each group. In classes for nursery and kindergarten children there should be at least two teachers in order to respond adequately to the needs of the children.

The Sunday School Time Schedule (Examples)

Effective teaching takes time, especially when methods of teaching are employed which are varied and allow for creative expressions of learnings.

Expanded Session Plan: Under this plan, in addition to the usual time allotted to the Sunday school, a part or all of the church worship hour is used, thereby extending the period of learning activity for the children. Thus, instead of only one hour, the children have from one and one-half hours to two and one-half hours, making possible a varied program of graded worship and teaching. Curriculum resources generally contain sufficient or optional material that can be utilized in the expanded time period.

United Program of the Church: Under this plan the church seeks to lead the children, youth, and adults of the church each Sunday morning through a united experience of worship and study. Everyone is expected to share in this balanced program, thereby eliminating the practice of having some persons come only to the

"Sunday school" and some only to "church." Because the duplication of worship and assembly programs is avoided in the youth and adult divisions, more time is available for study. The unified program usually uses the expanded session plan for the children.

See charts next page for sample time schedules.

Expanded Session

Nursery	Continuous Departmental Program (classes)		
Kindergarten	10:00 - 12:15		
Primary	Classes	Church Worship	Extended Session
Junior	10:00 - 11:00	11:15 - 11:45	11:45 - 12:15
Youth	Classes	Church Worship Service	
Adults	10:00 - 11:00	11:15 - 12:15	

United Program

Nursery	Continuous Departmental Program (classes)	
Kindergarten	10:00 - 12:15	
Primary	Church Worship Service	Sunday School Classes
Junior	10:00 - 10:30	10:35 - 12:15
Youth	Church Worship Service	Sunday School Classes
Adult	10:00 - 11:00	11:10 - 12:15

Identifying My Needs as a Teacher[11]

Instructions

Read the following items. Think of your own needs as a church school teacher. If you have a **great** need in an area, mark it with a **2**; if you have **some** need, mark it with a **1**; if you feel that you have **no** need in an area, then mark it with a **0**.

In order to be a more effective teacher, I need:

___ to understand more about the persons I teach

___ help in using the curriculum that is provided

___ the opportunity to study with other adults

___ guidelines to help me in planning lessons

___ skill in using the Bible and Bible study tools

___ help in asking questions and leading discussions

___ to know more about how to use audiovisuals

___ to know more about how to use music and art

___ more skill in telling stories

___ suggestions about dealing with behavior problems

___ skill in using the Bible with the students

___ other (state this need explicitly)

Notes

1. An excerpt from "A Curriculum Plan for the Church School," approved by the Curriculum Committee of the American Baptist Churches, January 10, 1968.

2. Louise B. Barger, *Growing Through the Sunday School: A Sourcebook for Sunday School Growth* (Valley Forge: American Baptist Churches of Pennsylvania and Delaware, n.d.), 1.

3. Kenneth D. Blazier and Linda R. Isham, ed., *The Teaching Church at Work: A Manual for the Board of Christian Education*, rev. (Valley Forge: Judson Press, 1993), 69-70. For more information about this study write Search Institute, 122 West Franklin Avenue, Minneapolis, MN 55404 or call 612/870-9511.

4. Barger, *Growing Through the Sunday School*, 1-2.

5. Appropriate portions adapted from "A Curriculum Plan for the Church School," approved by the Curriculum Committee of the American Baptist Churches, January 10, 1968.

6. Richard R. Hammar, Steven W. Klipowicz, and James F. Cobble, Jr., *Reducing the Risk of Child Sexual Abuse in Your Church* (Matthews, N.C.: Christian Ministry Resources, 1993), 11.

7. Evelyn M. Huber, *Enlist, Train, Support Church Leaders* (Valley Forge, Judson Press, 1975), 7.

8. Eugene C. Roehlkepartain, *The Teaching Church: Moving Christian Education to Center Stage* (Nashville: Abingdon Press, 1993), 93-94.

9. "Collection," the list prepared by Educational Ministries, ABC/USA may be obtained by calling 1-800-4-JUD-SON.

10. Kenneth D. Blazer and Linda R. Isham, *The Teaching Church at Work*, rev. (Valley Forge: Judson Press, 1993), 75-78.

11. Donald L. Griggs and Judy McKay Walther, *Christian Education in the Small Church* (Valley Forge: Judson Press, 1988), 60.